JOHN P. BOWMAN

SpringerBriefs in Law

D0721510

More information about this series at http://www.springer.com/series/10164

Raphael J. Heffron

Energy Law: An Introduction

 Springer

Raphael J. Heffron
School of Law and Centre for Integrated
 Energy Research
University of Leeds
Leeds
UK

Raphael J. Heffron
Associate Researcher, Energy Policy
 Research Group
University of Cambridge
Cambridge
UK

ISSN 2192-855X   ISSN 2192-8568 (electronic)
SpringerBriefs in Law
ISBN 978-3-319-14190-9   ISBN 978-3-319-14191-6 (eBook)
DOI 10.1007/978-3-319-14191-6

Library of Congress Control Number: 2014958134

Springer Cham Heidelberg New York Dordrecht London

Springer International Publishing AG Switzerland is part of Springer Science+Business Media
(www.springer.com)

Preface

The aim of this short text on *Energy Law: An Introduction* is simply to introduce the reader to this topic. It is intended for a global audience and rather than being restricted to potential energy law students, is written also for students of other disciplines such as geographers, social scientists, and engineers. It should also be engaging to those in a variety of professional practices who want an accessible background to and overview of the subject.

The text aims to outline the principles and central logic behind energy law. Therefore, readers from across the world should be able to use it as a guide to thinking about energy law in their own countries. A variety of examples from different countries are included in the text and while there is a majority focus on the EU and US, they represent good examples of more advanced and innovative energy law.

For those readers who seek further or more in-depth knowledge, this text will only serve as an introduction. They should look at the suggested extra readings and build from there.

The aim of the text is to introduce new readers to the developing area of energy law. The hope is that it provides an introduction to the legal challenges faced in the energy sector and the potential contribution of energy law to delivering a better world for the future generations.

October 2014

Raphael J. Heffron

Acknowledgments

I would like to thank all who contributed in some form to the development of this short text. I would like to thank those who introduced me to the energy sector at the University of Cambridge (UK) and in particular, Professor William Nuttall and Professor Angus Johnston. Thanks also to those at the various institutions where I built up knowledge of planning, environmental, and energy law and policy—these include the Energy Policy Research Group (University of Cambridge, UK), Massachusetts Institute of Technology (US), the University of Texas at Austin (US), the British Institute of International and Comparative Law (UK), the Honourable Society of King's Inns (Ireland), Trinity College Dublin (Ireland), University of St. Andrews (UK), University of Stirling (UK), and the University of Leeds (UK).

Sincere thanks also go to my family for their assistance and understanding, and the writing of this short text in Achill, Kas, Kazi, and Cambridge. And finally, this book is:

Le haghaidh mo bhean chéile agus mo h-oileán

Contents

About the Author

Raphael J. Heffron is a Lecturer in Law at the University of Leeds, United Kingdom. His research focuses centrally on on Energy Law and Policy. His other research interests include environmental law and climate change, planning law, law and strategy, tort, and law and technology.

Raphael read for his Ph.D. at Trinity Hall, University of Cambridge. He holds degrees from the University of Cambridge (MPhil), the University of St. Andrews (MLitt), and Trinity College Dublin (BA, MA). In the past he has held visiting positions at Massachusetts Institute of Technology, MA, USA (Visiting Student), The University of Texas at Austin, TX, USA (Visiting Scholar), and the British Institute for International and Comparative Law (Visiting Research Fellow).

Raphael is a trained Barrister-at-Law and was called to the Bar in July 2007 in the Republic of Ireland. He has acted as a consultant for the World Bank and for London thinktanks. Raphael is Associate Researcher of the Energy Policy Research Group at the University of Cambridge and a Policy Fellow, Policy Fellows Network, Centre for Science and Policy, also at the University of Cambridge. e-mail: r.j.heffron@leeds.ac.uk

Chapter 1
What Is Energy Law?

1.1 Introduction: What Is Energy Law?

Energy law concerns the management of energy resources. This is a simple defi-
nition, and disguises that it is arguably one of the more complex areas of law. It
demands that a scholar in the area engage with other disciplines to some degree,
such as politics, economics, geography, environmental sciences and engineering.

In 2015, energy law is still considered a new area of law. It appears not to have
the established academic literature base of other legal areas. However, this is to
misunderstand what energy law is. It has been in existence in different forms for
over a century. In the 1800s and early 1900s, there was legislation to manage
energy sectors such as coal and oil. These energy sources are known as fossil fuels
(along with gas) and form one of the two main categories of energy sources. The
other category is low-carbon energy sources which have been in development since
after the Second World War (1945) and consist of nuclear energy, hydropower,
wind, solar, biomass and several other minor renewable energy sources.

Energy law has now come to the fore. It is viewed with a holistic approach today
whereas before it was divided into many parts—in general in terms of each type of
energy source. There is a realisation in the twenty-first century of the fundamental role
that the energy sector plays in the economy of a country. It is an important sector for
employment, future economic development and the personal health of a nation's
citizens. In particular, it has been pushed high up the political agenda with the advent
of climate change and policies concerning energy security. For example, the impacts
of Russia's ability to affect gas prices in the majority of the European Union (EU) have
highlighted the importance of the energy sector at both EU and Member State level.
Further, politicians can be credited with pushing the agenda, in part, because high
energy prices—mainly electricity prices—have an influence on election outcomes.

It is no surprise therefore that, as a legal speciality, energy law has returned to
prominence. The area is now growing at an accelerated pace, with journals, textbooks
and practitioner books all appearing in numbers. Commercially, there is widespread

© The Author(s) 2015   1
R.J. Heffron, *Energy Law: An Introduction*,
SpringerBriefs in Law, DOI 10.1007/978-3-319-14191-6_1

growth of energy law divisions in the majority of medium to large legal practices. Legal training in energy law has also increased, with a proliferation of continuing professional development (CPD) summer courses and dedicated Masters courses, and a number of undergraduate law programmes in the EU and US have introduced it as a core and optional subject.

The European Union itself represents an example of the subject status of energy law. The EU was founded upon two treaties—the European Coal and Steel Community Treaty and the Euratom Treaty—that were used to manage the natural resources and energy assets of countries within the initial group of Member States. Indeed, the initial aim was to prevent—or at least limit—the possibility of future outbreaks of war by having a common management scheme for energy resources and assets. The two treaties that formed the EU—with one of these, the Euratom Treaty, unchanged since—are one reason why specific energy law did not appear in individual Member States until the last decade.

The next decade will be particularly important for the energy sector globally. The energy infrastructure built and policy concerning future energy infrastructure development during this period will determine whether many countries will meet the climate change targets that they set for the period 2020–2050 (considering the life-span of new energy infrastructure is generally 25 years plus), and they will set in place the physical and legal frameworks within which energy policy will have to function for many years.

A vital purpose of current energy law is to encourage, incentivise and/or initiate new energy infrastructure. For example, nearly a decade ago the United States enacted the Energy Policy Act 2005. The key aim of this piece of legislation was to initiate several hundred billion dollars worth of new energy infrastructure projects. While initially it was slow in its application, the Act has since 2012 resulted in almost $30 billion of energy projects beginning construction—in particular, the nuclear energy projects in the states of Georgia and South Carolina.

Similarly, the UK government declared that the goal of its Energy Act 2013 was to initiate £110 billion of new energy infrastructure. Across Europe, many countries plan to follow the UK approach to energy law in encouraging investment in energy infrastructure, and as such developments in energy law will be of considerable value and interest to policy-makers, practising lawyers and scholars across Europe. The development of energy infrastructure is seen as not only a method of increasing economic growth through spending, but also a key means of achieving future economic growth through developing energy infrastructure supply chains and exportable expertise and technology in the sector.

1.2 Scope of the Text

This chapter is a general introduction to energy law. It will provide a useful background to energy law for new students and is also accessible to those from other disciplines such as the social sciences, environmental sciences and engineering.

The text is formed of four parts. The first covers what energy law is, and includes an analysis of its key components, the key organisations and the key influences on the subject. The second part provides a background to the three levels of energy law, from international to national to local energy law. The third section of the text delves into more detail and examines energy law in the context of energy policy concepts and the overlap with environmental law. The section concludes with an examination of the law for different energy sources, both fossil fuel and low-carbon energy sources.

The fourth and final part of the chapter engages with the key research focus in the area of energy law, comparative energy law analysis and an introduction to some key case law in the area. The text concludes with a summary of potential future directions of energy law.

1.3 Elements of Energy Law

1.3.1 The Energy Law and Policy Triangle

It is hard to separate the study of energy law from energy policy. In many ways they are intertwined. The main theory in energy law and policy that this text offers can be seen simplistically in Fig. 1.1. Here this is referred to as the Energy Law and Policy Triangle and it is also known in other cases as the Energy Trilemma; either name can be used in the literature. However, it is advanced that there is a

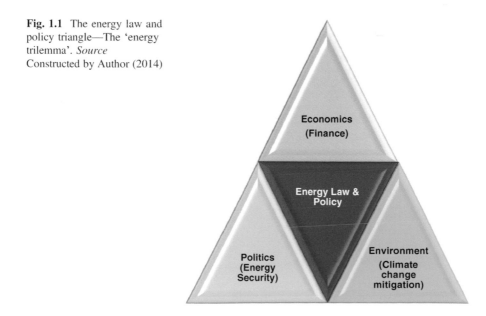

Fig. 1.1 The energy law and policy triangle—The 'energy trilemma'. *Source* Constructed by Author (2014)

distinction, as the challenge of balancing the energy law and policy triangle raises the question of the energy trilemma and how does society resolve it.

Energy law and policy is in the centre of the triangle and on the three points of the triangle are economics (finance), politics (energy security) and environment (climate change mitigation). These three issues are each trying to pull energy law and policy in their direction. In essence, effective and efficient energy law and policy will balance these three aims to deliver the best outcome to society. However, if one examines energy law and policy in more detail, often it is just one of these issues that dominates the energy agenda.

1.3.2 Energy Law Legislators

Energy law is derived from three levels of law, international, national and local. The first level can initially take the form of international treaties. These are global agreements signed by a number of countries on particular issues. Examples of some of these are listed in Table 1.1. These set out certain standards for a variety of activities in the energy sector.

The United Nations (UN) driven agreements on climate change have been ongoing since the Declaration of the United Nations Conference on the Human Environment, (adopted at Stockholm on 16 June 1972). Often these and following agreements are seen as international environmental treaties but they can also be described as energy-related. These international agreements now heavily influence what new energy infrastructure is built in countries that are signatories to the treaties. For example, many countries signed the Kyoto Protocol, which meant

Table 1.1 International treaties for energy issues	International treaties for energy issues
	• Vienna convention for the protection of the ozone layer (Vienna, 22 March 1985)
	• Montreal protocol on substances that deplete the ozone layer (Montreal, 16 September 1987)
	• United Nations framework convention on climate change (Rio, 9 May 1992)
	• Kyoto protocol to the United Nations framework convention on climate change (Kyoto, 11 December 1977)
	• Aarhus convention on access to information, public participation in decision-making and access to justice in environmental matters (Aarhus, 25 June 1988)
	• Convention on environmental impact assessment in a transboundary context (Espoo, 25 February 1991)
	• Lugano convention on civil liability for damages resulting from activities dangerous to the environment (Lugano, 21 June 1993-not yet in force)
	Source Constructed by Author (2014)

having to reduce their greenhouse gas emissions. In the UK, this in part prompted the move over the past decade to introduce legislation to promote more renewable energy development, with new development in fossil fuels not being a key feature of this new legislation.

The next level of energy law development can be seen in supranational administration. The EU and US are the prime examples here. In the EU, the EU Commission sets policy and legislative goals in the energy sector that are followed by 28 Member States, with a combined population of 507 million (Eurostat 2014). Similarly the US sets Federal policy and law for its 50 states and has a population of 316 million (US Census Bureau 2013). While these two essentially federal governments represent a minority of the world's population, they lead the international community in setting energy law and policy. Many other countries look to these two regions for guidance in establishing new energy law and policy in their respective states.

The key source of energy law and policy is national governments. Governments set the energy policy in their country and then introduce the legislation to meet those goals. Many Member States in the EU and states in the US have to take into account federal law and policy but these states have a large amount of autonomy as to how they meet their energy needs. Other countries outside the EU and US are generally free to set their own energy law and policy but have to take into account whatever international treaties they may be signatories to. For many countries, issues such as international political and trade relationships with other countries also influence their energy law and policy formulation.

The final place where energy law and policy is developed is at a local level. This is where local legislators from regions to small counties (or districts) set certain energy goals and may offer local incentives for companies that plan to develop energy infrastructure in their region. These usually take the form of tax breaks, grants and the transfer of land. An example is Victoria County in the state of Texas in the US where Exelon was given benefits for initially developing its plans to build a new nuclear plant there.

1.3.3 Energy Law and Policy Organisations

There are a number of energy law and policy organisations that provide analysis, new approaches and perspectives on energy policy in an international context. Table 1.2 lists these key organisations.

Table 1.2 is not a complete listing of all the key energy law and policy organisations. However, it is a list of the most influential organisations, which also make a significant amount of published material available free to all readers. The EU, UN and US Department of Energy produce numerous policy documents and hold copies of legislation and international treaties. The energy research centres at the Universities of Oxford and Cambridge are very strong at producing publications on issues across the energy sector and with an international context. The energy centre

Table 1.2 The main energy law and policy organisations

Energy law and policy organisations
1. International Energy Agency http://www.worldenergyoutlook.org/
2. International Atomic Energy Agency http://www.iaea.org/
3. United Nations Environmental Programme http://www.undp.org/content/undp/en/home/ourwork/ environmentandenergy/overview.html
4. European Commission Energy Department http://ec.europa.eu/energy/index_en.htm
5. Department of Energy, US http://www.energy.gov/
6. Oxford Energy Institute, University of Oxford, UK http://www.oxfordenergy.org/
7. Energy Policy Research Group, University of Cambridge, UK http://www.eprg.group.cam.ac.uk/
8. MIT Center for Energy and Environmental Research, US http://web.mit.edu/ceepr/www/
9. Centre for Energy, Petroleum, and Mineral Law and Policy, University of Dundee, UK http://www.dundee.ac.uk/cepmlp/

Source Constructed by Author (2014)

at MIT has long had an influence in providing input into US energy policy, and it is noticeable that one of its members, Professor Ernest Moniz, was appointed as the Secretary of State for Energy in the Barack Obama administration in May 2013. There are many other energy research centres in other countries but they have not yet the capacity and volume of publications that these aforementioned centres have.

1.3.4 Influences on Energy Law

Numerous other areas of the law influence energy law. It is vital for the energy law student to be aware of the effect of changes in these other areas of law that affect the energy sector; a brief overview will be provided here, and this will be explored in more detail in Chap. 3.

The first of these areas is environmental law. Energy law and environmental law are intertwined and both have similar characteristics, and are concerned with legislating for the effective management of natural resources. However, in the case of energy law, the natural resources with which it is concerned are those that can yield energy directly, or possess the potential to do so, and thereby contribute to electricity production. Hence, major concerns of environmental law, such as forestry, habitat and wildlife, are not a focus of energy law. Nevertheless, the link between them is obvious given the potential of energy assets to threaten forestry, habitat or wildlife, either by their location or as a result of their pollution.

The importance of energy law and environmental law is in providing legislation to manage the natural resources of a country, and in their potential for changing human and societal behaviour; another important characteristic is that of policy formulation. Both energy and environmental law demonstrate to a greater extent than other areas of the law the interchange between law and policy and the importance of policy-makers. Policy development drives forward energy and environmental law. Environmental law has at its core an international agenda that informs and pushes regions to implement the various international treaties and consequently to legislate for these. Energy law too is affected by national energy policy, which in turn is driven by international agreements or targets.

Related to the influence of environmental law are planning and construction law. Both these areas of law affect the development of energy infrastructure. For example, many countries have specific planning law relating to energy infrastructure development. This legislation will in general call for accelerated decision-making on planning applications for new energy infrastructure. In addition, the scale of energy projects has implications for local communities, and as a result there is applicable planning law regarding public participation in the planning process. Construction law is more standard as legislation and will apply similarly to energy projects as it does to other large infrastructure projects, such as transport and other public infrastructure.

Energy law is also influenced increasingly by other disciplines. These include, in particular, strategy, project management, finance and economics. These subjects influence, in essence, the ambition of the energy sector and what it can achieve given the constraints imposed by these disciplines. The level of their influence is determined by the strength of the actor groups associated with each discipline. Economists are influential in terms of differentiating the respective costs and benefits of building different energy infrastructure for the different energy sources—using, in general, cost benefit analysis (CBA). Economists have also played a key role in determining the structure of the electricity market, and therefore which type of energy infrastructure has been developed.

Energy law is beginning to be more holistic in its approach. For example, included in energy law legislation now are various issues previously associated with these other areas of law, such as subsidy mechanisms, health and safety issues, and liability issues.

1.3.5 International Drivers of Change in Energy Law

As well as understanding the key influences on energy law and policy it is important to know why energy law may change. The drivers of change in energy law can be complex and arise mainly at international and national levels.

Change begins with *international treaties*. Many of these are well established (examples of some of these appear in Table 1.1) and when they are updated they prompt change in national energy law.

International agencies also drive change. An example of this is the International Atomic Energy Agency (IAEA). The IAEA can set new law and policy guidelines for the international nuclear energy sector, and countries that are members have to change their nuclear energy law and policy as a result. An example of this is safety practices and insurance (liability) in the nuclear energy sector (which will be discussed later at Sect. 3.3). Similarly there are agencies (for example, the International Association of Oil and Gas Producers) responsible for offshore oil and gas safety practices, and, again, countries change their national energy law to take into account new policies proposed by these agencies.

International politics (*relations*) is also a driver of change. Countries often have highly developed political relationships that lead to cooperation on energy infrastructure development. This can take many forms but usually involves one country selling its energy expertise or technology to another country. An example of this is the developing international political relationship between Russia and Turkey. In the context of energy, this has resulted in Russia being given approval to build a four reactor nuclear plant at Akkuyu in Turkey. Russia will build and then own and operate the plant for 20 years before selling it to Turkey. Similarly, Romania built a nuclear power plant in a consortium with a Canadian nuclear energy company and availed itself of Canadian expertise during the project and after the plant was operational.

Linked with international politics as a driver of change in energy law is *international business and trade*. Often energy projects such as the ones mentioned above result from and include agreements on other international business and trade between two countries. These agreements for the sale of other products (usually non-energy products) can see one country being given the contract to build energy infrastructure, and energy law and policy will change as a result.

1.3.6 National Drivers of Change in Energy Law

There are a number of drivers of change at national level. These are related to some degree to the international drivers. The *Aim of Government* is the first of these. This is of importance as, depending on the political party in government, energy policy may be subject to change. From the examples in Table 1.3, it is evident that the election of a new government can result in significant changes in energy law and policy.

Related to the *Aim of Government* are *Availability of Finance*; *Advances in Technology*; and *Societal Preferences*. These are issues a government has to consider when formulating its own energy policy. However, they are also issues in their own right. The *Availability of Finance* has been particularly important since the beginning of the financial crisis in 2007. Obtaining finance for a project has become

Table 1.3 New governments and new energy law

Germany
With the election of Angela Merkel's government in 2005, energy policy in Germany changed. The energy policy promoted by her party and government involved a significant emphasis on renewable energy development and the closure of nuclear energy plants—which did receive an impetus after the Fukushima accident in Japan in 2011
United Kingdom
The indecision of the UK coalition government elected in May 2010 has delayed new investment in the UK energy sector. It took the first few years of the government for both parties (the Conservatives and the Liberal Democrats) to agree a way forward. This indecision has reduced the interest from investors in the UK energy sector, and there has been little interest in developing new energy infrastructure
France
Since the election of François Hollande of the French socialist party as president of France in May 2012, French energy policy has changed. The previous dominance of nuclear energy within the French energy policy is being reduced and a new emphasis has been placed on renewable energy development, with a planned limit on the use of nuclear energy to 50 % of the country's energy mix by 2025

Source Constructed by Author (2014)

increasingly difficult and investors are looking for a guaranteed return on their investment. Energy projects can be seen as risky. Some suffer from long construction times and others from long planning processes, and this increases the risk profile of each project. In a time of recession, investors will look for more secure projects. There have been many cases where investors have pulled out from completing major energy projects—see Table 1.4 for examples.

In many cases where the *Availability of Finance* is an issue, new energy law and policy will be formulated that will have as one of its objectives to increase the investment in the energy sector. For example, and as stated previously, the specific aim of the UK Energy Act 2013 was to stimulate £110 billion in investment in the energy sector. Its success in achieving this will determine when new legislation will be introduced in the future.

Advances in Technology will also contribute to change in energy law. Advances in the technology for wind turbines and solar energy are having a major effect in many countries. This has resulted in many countries changing their energy law in part to capture these technological benefits from more efficient technology—Denmark and Germany are good examples of this. This is also currently evident in relation to Carbon Capture and Storage (CCS) technology. The advances made in this technology may see a return of new coal-fired plants that use this technology. Energy law has been changed to promote the use of CCS technology, for example, in the US and the UK.

Table 1.4 Energy projects
and investor withdrawal

Romania
Originally there were six investors involved in building Romania's third and fourth nuclear reactors; however, in 2009 three of these withdrew. Another investor withdrew in 2012, and the final two had done so by December 2013
United Kingdom
Numerous wind energy projects have been cancelled (for example, the Atlantic Array £4 billion wind farm project). The investors RWE stated that there were financial considerations in their decisions

Source Constructed by Author (2014)

A final related driver of change in energy law is *Societal Preferences*. Different countries have different societal structures which contribute in part to different societal preferences. In many cases, this emanates from how the culture has developed over time. For example, the Republic of Ireland has a very anti-nuclear stance. For the Republic of Ireland to build a nuclear reactor, there would have to be a referendum on the issue in which every individual would have a vote. This is in contrast to the UK where the majority of the population still see nuclear energy as part of the UK energy mix and a solution to reducing CO_2 emissions (Pidgeon et al. 2008; Poortinga et al. 2013). In France nuclear expertise and technology was developed to the degree that engineers had a dominant role in energy policy formulation for several decades. In Denmark there has been cross-party political support for the development of wind energy since the 1970s and this has resulted in a society that sees wind energy as the solution to its energy problem and a way to reduce its reliance on fossil fuels, and also as a contributor to economic development. In the US certain states have a culture that has developed around their coal-mining industry. It is hard in such communities to break the preference of some citizens to continue with coal mining and coal-fired plants.

1.3.7 Local/Individual Theory of Change in Energy Law

In examining the drivers of change for energy law and policy, it is possible to construct a theory of change in energy law and policy from an individual perspective. This can be seen in Fig. 1.2 where there are three intertwining perspectives: a world perspective, a national perspective and a local perspective. The world perspective is supported by a cosmopolitan philosophy where individuals view themselves as world citizens and view prospective change as enabling change for the better of humanity. This takes the form of the development of international treaties and is led by international institutions. The national perspective is where the individuals have voted politicians into government, and governments in turn apply their political mandate to bring in new energy law and policy—as such, this

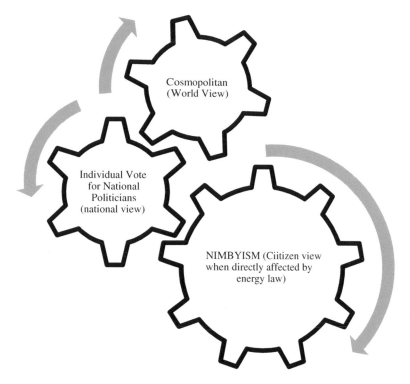

Fig. 1.2 Individual theory of change in energy law. *Source* Constructed by Author (2014)

perspective is national government led. The local perspective is where individuals form their views on energy policy when they are directly impacted by it. The view of individuals here is affected by their personal finances, the health effects resulting from energy infrastructure, and the location of energy infrastructure. In the last of these, the location of energy infrastructure, NIMBYism (Not-in-my back-yard) syndrome is of concern, and results in public participation at a local level, with people giving their views on energy infrastructure development located near to their places of residence.

1.3.8 Conclusion

Energy law is not a legal subject that is as conclusive as, for example, tax (revenue) law. It is one that will continuously evolve and/or be renewed. It is important therefore for students of energy law to think critically and to aim to identify the strengths and weaknesses of the energy law of whichever countries they choose to study.

Students need to know the energy law and policy of a particular country. They should be able to detail its application and whether it is successfully achieving its aims. The key institutions at international, national and local levels are of direct relevance to the study of energy law. Students need to learn the dynamics of the energy sector in examining the roles of different institutions and thus build evidence to support their answers.

1.3.9 Final Reflections

Understand and consider the following:

- **What is energy law?**
- **Sources of energy**
- **Energy law terminology and key energy sector actors**

1.4 Recommended Reading

This list is by no means complete but should provide the reader with a good start to developing their knowledge of the area.

1. Barton, B, Redgwell, C, Rønne, A and Zillman, DN (eds) (2004) Energy security: managing risk in a dynamic legal and regulatory environment. Oxford, United Kingdom, Oxford University Press
2. Cameron, P (2nd ed) (2007) Competition in energy markets: law and regulation in the European Union. Oxford, United Kingdom, Oxford University Press
3. Cameron, P (ed) (2005) Legal aspects of EU energy regulation: implementing the new directives on electricity and gas across Europe. Oxford, United Kingdom, Oxford University Press.
4. Cameron, P (2005) International energy investment law: the pursuit of stability. Oxford, United Kingdom, Oxford University Press
5. Delvaux, B (2013) EU law and the development of a sustainable, competitive and secure energy policy: opportunity and shortcomings. Cambridge, UK, Intersentia
6. Johnston, A and Block, G (2012) EU energy law. Oxford, UK, Oxford University Press
7. Park, P (2013) (2nd ed) International law for energy and the environment. Florida, US, CRC Press, Taylor and Francis

8. RoggenKamp, M, Redgwell, C, Rønne, A and Del Gyayo, I (eds) (2007) Energy law in Europe, national, EU and international regulation. Oxford, UK, Oxford University Press
9. Talus, K (inspired by Thomas Wälde) (2013) EU energy law and policy: a critical account. Oxford, United Kingdom, Oxford University Press
10. Talus, K (ed) (2014) Research handbook on international energy law. Cheltenham, UK, Edward Elgar

It is also worth reading the eight-volume Claeys & Casteels Series on EU Energy Law, http://www.claeys-casteels.com/series_eu_energy_law.php

References

Eurostat (2014) Population data. http://epp.eurostat.ec.europa.eu/tgm/table.do?tab=table&language=en&pcode=tps00001&tableSelection=1&footnotes=yes&labeling=labels&plugin=1. Accessed 18 Oct 2014

Pidgeon NF, Lorenzoni I, Poortinga W (2008) Climate change or nuclear power—no thanks! A quantitative study of public perceptions and risk framing in Britain. Glob Environ Change 18:69–85

Poortinga W, Aoyagi M, Pidgeon NF (2013) Public perceptions of climate change and energy futures before and after the Fukushima accident: a comparison between Britain and Japan. Energy Policy 62:1204–1211

US Census Bureau (2013) United States census bureau people QuickFacts. http://quickfacts.census.gov/qfd/states/00000.html. Accessed 18 Oct 2014

Chapter 2
The Different Levels of Energy Law

2.1 International Energy Law

2.1.1 Introduction

To recap from Chap. 1 of the text, energy law has three distinct levels. These take the form of energy law at international, national and local level. At international level there are international treaties, initially formulated by international institutions. The main relevant international institutions in the energy sector are the United Nations (UN), the World Bank, the European Union (EU) and the International Atomic Energy Agency (IAEA). These institutions focus on different aspects.

The UN has long had a focus on environmental issues. As a result, it has contributed to change in the energy sector, particularly in terms of being responsible for international climate change agreements. The UN has a division called the UN Environment Programme (UNEP) which is responsible for environmental issues. Recently, however, the UNEP has increased its scope to include energy issues and it now has several sub-divisions that focus on energy issues. The UNEP is also engaging with the energy sector through funding research. For example, the Global Subsidies Initiative (GSI) is being supported in some of its activities by the UNEP; the GSI calculates the estimated amounts that different energy sources receive in energy subsidies across the world. Similarly the World Bank has endorsed and initially funded the Extractive Industries Transparency Initiative (EITI); the EITI is an international agreement whereby countries record how much companies pay their governments for the rights to extract energy resources.

The World Bank plays an interesting role in the international energy sector. It is an institution interested in developing trade and enabling less developed countries to grow their economies. In many cases it is the World Bank that provides loans for less developed countries to build their energy infrastructure. In addition, it supports countries that are creating and renewing their energy law so as to accommodate new energy infrastructure and the reform of their energy sector. The World Bank therefore

© The Author(s) 2015
R.J. Heffron, *Energy Law: An Introduction*,
SpringerBriefs in Law, DOI 10.1007/978-3-319-14191-6_2

plays a significant role in the formation of energy law and policy in many developing countries. It achieves this through a number of its individual divisions, for example the International Finance Corporation and the International Bank for Reconstruction and Development.

The EU has a major role in the international energy sector. It develops its own energy law and policy for its Member States. Many countries across the world look to the EU and its Member States for guidance and inspiration in creating their own energy law and policy. The EU has a triple focus of energy security, environment and competition in terms of energy law and policy development. Several parts of the EU are concerned with the energy sector. The first of these is the European Commission Energy Department (Directorate-General) which formulates new energy law and policy. Several other EU institutions also play a role, including the European Parliament, the European Agency for the Cooperation of Energy Regulators, and Euratom.

Many other international institutions play a role in the energy sector. One of the most influential in terms of the international energy sector is the International Atomic Energy Agency (IAEA). The IAEA plays a lead role in the international nuclear energy industry. There is no similar international organisation for other energy sources. The IAEA is located in Vienna, Austria, and 162 countries are currently Member States. It acts as an international driver of the nuclear energy sector, and it has a particular focus on maintaining the safe operation of nuclear energy plants across the world.

The IAEA is responsible for ensuring what are, in essence, global safety standards for the industry. It also gives law and policy advice, in order that countries adopting specific law related to nuclear energy develop nuclear energy infrastructure in the safest possible way. The IAEA plays a role also in the event of an accident. The main action by the IAEA in this context is its promotion of a liability regime for nuclear accidents. This encompasses a number of international treaties on nuclear liability. There are three main international liability agreements and the members of IAEA are all signed up to one or more of these three agreements. The three main agreements are the Paris Convention, the Brussels Convention, and the Convention of Supplementary Compensation for Nuclear Damage.

The IAEA is an example of worldwide cooperation in one area of the energy sector. It has not being achieved for another energy source. The interesting question therefore is: why can it not be achieved for other energy sources? Further, what would be the benefits of more international cooperation on the development and safety of other energy sources? These are areas of further research and ones on which a student of energy law should develop a critical perspective.

2.1.2 Ruling Courts

There are a number of international ruling courts in the energy sector. These are listed below in order of importance. These courts are becoming increasingly influential in the energy sector. In particular, decisions from the Energy Charter Treaty are increasing in prominence and influencing the behaviour of energy firms in the energy sector.

The UN General Assembly: This is where debate begins on international energy issues. Formative energy policies are developed and deliberated upon here. Decisions require a two-thirds majority.

International Court of Justice: This is the judicial organ of the UN. It settles legal disputes submitted by states and offers legal opinions on selected issues. A common energy issue submitted to the court may concern ownership of offshore oil and gas fields.

International Chamber of Commerce (ICC)—International Court of Arbitration: This is the leading international organisation for the resolution of international disputes by arbitration. It also has a research office.

Energy Charter Treaty (ECT): For the energy sector it is increasingly through the ECT that international energy disputes are resolved. The ECT aims to strengthen the rule of law in the international energy sector so as to ensure a level playing field for all governments and to reduce the risk involved in cross-border trade and investment.

European Court of Justice (ECJ): The ECJ determines rulings on energy issues within the EU. It has a significant effect on the European energy sector and prompts change in energy law and therefore company behaviour. The volume of cases in energy law is increasing. In some cases, firms change their behavior to avoid an ECJ judgment. More detailed analysis of ECJ decisions is covered in Chap. 4.

Specific treaties: There are specific treaties that while they cannot be technically classed as a 'ruling court', do in essence have some of the responsibilities associated with a 'ruling court'. For instance, a number of the international treaties listed in Table 1.1 require annual reports. For example, the Basel Convention on the Control of Transboundary Movements of Hazardous Wastes requires an annual report. The effect of this annual report is to ensure that countries adhere to the terms of the Convention. However, in relation to the enforcement of several treaties in the nuclear energy sector, it is also the IAEA that enforces these treaties with inspection trips to these countries.

2.1.3 Elements of International Law

Many elements of international law apply to the energy sector. *Governance and formulation of energy policy* begins at international level and, as detailed earlier, has to adhere not just to relevant international treaties but also to the general principles of international law. There are also the *rights and obligations of States* under international law. In relation to the energy sector, these in particular concern transboundary issues, which include operations at sea (law of the sea).

Transboundary issues are numerous and are important in the context of accidents in the energy sector. Accidents in the nuclear energy sector and offshore oil and gas generally have transboundary effects. In addition, all operations at sea for energy sources can have potential transboundary issues. Law of the sea (sometimes referred to as maritime law) is itself a distinct area of law. In the context of the energy sector it refers to the transport and control of hazardous wastes (such as nuclear waste) and also offshore oil and gas drilling.

A major issue at international energy law level is compliance and enforcement. As stated earlier, the nuclear energy industry is more globally regulated than other areas, as a result of the work of the IAEA. But for other energy sources compliance and enforcement are bigger challenges. There are mechanisms such as the Extractive Industries Transparency Initiative (which focuses on information disclosure) for mining, but the key mechanism is the Energy Charter Treaty or resolutions found in the International Commercial Court. Other mechanisms for compliance and enforcement may be the World Bank, the IMF or the European Bank for Reconstruction and Development (EBRD) which lend money to energy projects and may attach terms and conditions to them.

Energy infrastructure development can impact upon environmental protection and conservation. At an international level, the UN plays a lead role in this case. There are two issues here, the protection of the environment and heritage management. The UN achieves both. First, it does so through a multitude of different treaties which are detailed earlier in Table 1.1. Secondly, it governs heritage management through heritage law and policy treaties that manage other conservation and protection efforts—see Table 2.1 for a list of the international legislation in the area relevant to energy infrastructure construction.

2.1.4 International Energy Law Specific to Energy Sources

This section re-emphasises the international energy law that is specific to each energy source. Evident in Table 2.2 is the fact there are international energy law issues for the oil, gas, coal and nuclear energy sectors. This is not the case for renewable energy sources. Renewable energy development is more a national and local energy law issue. Energy law for different energy sources is examined in more detail in Chap. 3.

Table 2.1 International Heritage Law

International Heritage Law
• Convention on the Means of Prohibiting and Preventing the Illicit Import, Export and Transfer of Ownership of Cultural Property, 1970
• Convention concerning the Protection of the World Cultural and Natural Heritage, 1972
• Convention on the Protection of the Underwater Cultural Heritage, 2001
• Convention for the Safeguarding of the Intangible Cultural Heritage, 2003
• Convention on the Protection and Promotion of the Diversity of Cultural Expressions, 2005.

Source Constructed by Author (2014)

Table 2.2 International Energy Law

International Energy Law Specific to Energy Sources
• United Nations Convention on the Law of the Sea (UNCLOS) (Montego Bay, 10 December 1982)
• Basel Convention on the Control of Transboundary Movements of Hazardous Wastes and their Disposal (Basel, 22 March 1989)
• International Convention on Civil Liability for Oil Pollution Damage (Brussels, 29 November 1969)
• Convention on Early Notification of a Nuclear Accident, International Atomic Energy Agency, 1986
• Convention on Assistance in the Case of a Nuclear Accident or Radiological Emergency, International Atomic Energy Agency, 1986
• Energy Charter Treaty, 17 December 1994
• International Convention for the Prevention of Pollution from Ships 1973, as modified by the Protocol of 1978 (MARPOL)
• Treaty Establishing the European Atomic Energy Community, 25 March 1957
• 1960 Paris Convention on Nuclear Third Party Liability ("Paris Convention")
• 2004 Protocol to amend the Paris Convention on Nuclear Third Party Liability
• 1963 Brussels Supplementary Convention on Nuclear Third Party Liability ("Brussels Supplementary Convention")
• 2004 Protocol to amend the Brussels Supplementary Convention on Third Party Liability
• 1963 Vienna Convention on Civil Liability for Nuclear Damage ("Vienna Convention")
• 1997 Protocol to Amend the Vienna Convention on Civil Liability for Nuclear Damage
• 1988 Joint Protocol Relating to the Application of the Vienna Convention and the Paris Convention ("Joint Protocol")
• 1997 Convention on Supplementary Compensation for Nuclear Damage

Source Constructed by Author (2014)

2.1.5 Enforcement in International Energy Law

Enforcement is a major issue in international energy law as, in general, international law is more reactive than proactive. This is the case in international energy law also. The issue of enforcement has been mentioned earlier in Sect. 2.1.3 but this section examines it in relation to post-accident behaviour so in essence the level to which safety laws and practice are observed. The responses to the major energy accidents have been reactionary. Two recent major cases of this are the BP Deepwater Horizon oil spill disaster in the US (2010) and the Fukushima accident in Japan (2011). Forcing those responsible to compensate the victims of these two accidents and updating international laws post-accidents have been, and are, very slow processes. For example, since these accidents there have been limited updates applied to liability regimes for both nuclear and offshore oil and gas. Further, in the case of both accidents, those responsible are still in the process of compensating victims, with BP even disputing the amount they should compensate.

Table 2.3 Summary of severe accidents (≥5 fatalities) per energy chain and country group for the period 1970–2008

Energy chain	OECD		EU 27		Non-OECD	
	Accidents	Fatalities	Accidents	Fatalities	Accidents	Fatalities
Coal	87	2,259	45	989	2394[a]	38,672
					162	5,788
					818	11,302
					1214	15,750
Oil	187	3,495	65	1,243	358	19,156
Natural gas	109	1,258	37	367	78	1,556
LPG	58	1,856	22	571	70	2,789
Hydro	1[b]	14	1[c]	116	9[d]	3,961
					12	26,108[e]
Nuclear[f]	–	–	–	–	1	31
Biofuel	–	–	–	–	–	–
Biogas	–	–	–	–	2	18
Geothermal	–	–	–	–	1	21

Source Constructed and adapted by Author (2014) from Burgherr and Hirschberg (2014) Comparative Risk Assessment of Severe Accidents in the Energy Sector. Energy Policy (Advanced Access—doi: 10.1016/j.enpol.2014.01.035) with permission
[a] First line non-OECD total; second line non-OECD without China; third line China 1994–1999; fourth line China 2000–2008
[b] Teton dam failure (USA 1976)
[c] Belci dam failure (Romania 1991)
[d] First line non-OECD without China; second line China
[e] Banqiao/Shimantan dam failures (China 1975) together caused 26,000 fatalities
[f] Only immediate fatalities of the Chernobyl accident are shown here

There remain a high amount of accidents in the international energy sector industry. An examination of Table 2.3 reveals that a very substantial majority occur in the fossil fuel sector.

2.1.6 Connection to National Energy Law

International energy law has a major influence on national energy law, as stated earlier in this section. However, there are also significant differences in that states have a degree of autonomy in how they meet their international commitments. This makes the study of energy law very interesting and means that comparative studies on energy law in different countries are common. Students of energy law should not limit themselves in their research work to one-country case study research papers. It is necessary to always place the national energy law of one country in the context of both international energy law and the national energy law of one or more other countries.

2.1.7 Final Reflections

Understand and consider the following:

- **What are the key elements of international energy law?**
- **What are the key 'influential' international institutions?**
- **Distinguish the key features of international energy law**

2.2 National Energy Law

2.2.1 National Competing Demands

National energy law is subject to national competing demands. These follow the energy law and policy triangle (see Fig. 1.1). The formulation of national energy law depends on influences from economics, politics and the environment. Different countries direct their focus on these three factors of influence in different ways. Some countries achieve a better balance than others; hence the view of the energy law and policy triangle as the energy trilemma. It should also be remembered that countries have different energy mixes, and this can result in a different emphasis for energy law formulation. Examples of this are given in the next section.

2.2.2 Three Examples of National Energy Law and Policy

United Kingdom

The UK continues to plan to develop a nuclear programme consisting of, potentially, eight reactors, and of central importance to this is the Energy Act of 2013. This law is not solely based on initiating new nuclear energy infrastructure in the UK but includes legislation for developing renewable energy and unconventional oil and gas. This legislation is also designed specifically to transform the electricity market and to promote a low-carbon generation mix. It includes a number of key measures:

- to introduce Contracts for Difference (CfDs) to stabilise revenues for investors in low-carbon electricity generating projects;
- the introduction of a Capacity Market to further develop energy security;
- a Final Investment Decision (FID) that will allow early energy infrastructure projects to claim subsidies in advance of the legislation being introduced; and
- the continuation of the establishment of the Carbon Price Floor that provides a minimum price for carbon in the carbon market.

United States

The most recent key legislation in the US is the Energy Policy Act of 2005. There was also the Energy Independence and Security Act of 2007 but this was not as influential and it builds on what was contained in the 2005 Act. The Energy Policy Act of 2005 has provided some inspiration for the development of the Energy Act 2013 in the UK. One of the main aims of the Energy Policy Act of 2005 is to initiate nuclear energy infrastructure development in the US. In 2012 two nuclear projects received permission from the US Nuclear Regulatory Commission. These were the first licences granted in the US in 33 years and were awarded to:

- Plant Vogtle, Georgia—Combined Construction and Operating Licence granted February 2012 (AP1000 × 2); and
- V. C. Summer, South Carolina—Combined Construction and Operating Licence granted March 2012 (AP1000 × 2).

The Energy Policy Act of 2005 has other key aims also. There are benefits to other low-carbon energy sources as well as fossil fuels—see Table 2.4 for more details.

Table 2.4 Selection of incentives from the Energy Policy Act of 2005

Issue	Incentive offered
Construction risk (S. 638)	Offers risk assurance to cover 100 % of delays (up to $500 million) for the first two nuclear plants and 50 % of delays (up to $250 million) for plants three to six
Insurance (Title VI, Subtitle A)	The Price-Anderson Act, the insurance regime that applies to the civil nuclear energy sector, is extended for a further 20 years
Loan guarantee System (Title XVII)	Creation of new loan guarantee office for any clean energy technologies. Authorises loan guarantee (up to 80 % of project cost for nuclear) but also for IGCC (Integrated gasification combined cycle) plants and renewable energy projects, hydrogen fuel cell technology, carbon capture and sequestration projects, and the construction of refineries for gasoline, ethanol and biodiesel
Production tax credits (S. 1306)	Production tax credit of 1.8 cents per kilowatt-hour for 6,000 megawatts of capacity from nuclear power plants for the first eight years of operation. Wind and closed loop biomass have received a production tax credit since 1992 and received a further extension of this (S. 1301 for federal land projects)
Permit process (S. 365)	Permitting process for oil and gas was streamlined and this cuts out years and months of delays in a western states pilot programme—it will bring new gas and oil to the market sooner. S. 366 even states it is possible for a permit to drill to be issued within 30 days—though this is for a pilot project across western states only

Source Constructed by the author as of October 2011 from US Nuclear Regulatory Commission statistics (2011)

China

The Chinese government announced a new White Paper on Energy Policy in 2012. This new policy aims to see major investment in low-carbon energy infrastructure with wind power to reach 100 GWe, solar power to exceed 21 GWe and installed nuclear energy to be circa 40 GWe, all by the end of 2015. This energy policy is very ambitious and whether it achieves its aims is open to question. China has, however, began to develop a new electricity network (grid) infrastructure that will accommodate renewable energy. Developments in this regard may be significant for the growth of the renewable energy industry and prompt substantial decreases in the cost of renewable energy infrastructure development.

2.2.3 Formulation of National Energy Law

In the previous section, the influence of international energy law on national energy law was discussed. National energy law is subject to these international energy law commitments but how these are written into national energy law can vary from country to country. Further, national energy law has to take into account existing energy law, the respective national energy mix and energy resources, and the policy of the political party in government. These will be the key determinants of future energy law and policy.

Countries have their own systems for the formulation of energy law but in general this follows the methods for the formulation of law in other areas. There is a national consultation and the formation of a Green Paper, which is followed by another round of consultation and then the publication of a White Paper. The White Paper is discussed in Parliament (or similar) before energy experts are called to give evidence before a select committee of elected representatives. Additions and deletions occur before the White Paper is agreed upon and moved on to be the Energy Bill (or similar equivalent). The Energy Bill is then be presented and debated in Parliament and final amendments made before Parliament votes on whether it is to be passed into law. This process can take 1–3 years in many countries.

Energy law can also be enacted through additions to other legislation, as was previously mentioned (see Sect. 1.3.4), with additions to, for example, planning law and environmental law. There can also be cooperation by political parties on energy policy. This happens in Denmark where there is cross-party agreement on energy policy with a medium to long-term perspective.

It should be noted that political parties in general form their own energy policy and if they are elected, this energy policy forms the majority of the new energy policy of that country. However, political parties are influenced by particular political lobby groups and, inevitably, industries that give them financial donations; and hence these private sector companies and lobbyists can play a role in energy law and policy formulation.

2.2.4 The Energy and Electricity Mix

The energy and electricity mixes are vital information for the student of energy law. This usually determines the key aims of new energy law. The energy mix usually refers to the total amounts of each energy source consumed in a country, whereas the electricity mix concerns the electricity sector. The energy mix includes the energy used in other sectors such as transport.

Table 2.5 shows the energy mix of the UK, US and China. It is important in any assessment that a student includes such a table in relation the countries being studied. The table should always include the countries under assessment and a few others for comparison.

In the UK a key goal of the new Energy Act 2013 is to develop a low-carbon economy. Through a brief look at the energy mix of the UK, one can determine that fossil fuels account for 63.8 % of the electricity production. To keep the UK within its climate change targets, there needs to be action on reducing its reliance on fossil fuels and on movement towards low-carbon sources. As a result, this is the clear aim of the recent Energy Act 2013. Energy law in the US and China aims also to move these countries to low-carbon economies and, as a result, to reduce the reliance on fossil fuels—in particular the use of coal which is high in both countries.

2.2.5 Energy Finance Versus Pollution Control

There is much debate in the formulation of energy law and policy about the balance achieved between energy finance and pollution control. Usually the costs of energy projects are compared to each other. In Table 2.6 they are measured in price per kilowatt hour. There is significant debate in academic literature as to the merit of these evaluations. Often they do not include the full costing for pollution control. Without accurate costing, projects are valued differently and therefore this influences

Table 2.5 Electricity Mix (by Generation) in the UK, US and China

Energy source	UK (2013) (%)	US (2013) (%)	China (2012) (%)	Your country
Coal	36.3	39	66	?
Oil	0.7	<1	2	?
Gas	26.8	27	3	?
Hydropower	–	7	22	?
Renewables	14.8	4	5	?
Nuclear	19.8	19	1	?
Other renewables	1.5	1	1	?

Source Compiled and adapted by the Author (2014) from the following sources: DECC (2014), EPA (2014), and US EIA (2014a, b)

Table 2.6 Estimated levelised cost of electricity (LCOE) for new generation resources 2019 in the US

Plant Type	Capacity factor (%)	Levelised capital costs	Fixed operating and management	Variable operating and management (inc. fuel)	Trans-mission investment	Total system LCOE	Subsidy	Total LCOE inc. subsidy
Conventional coal	85	60.0	4.2	30.3	1.2	95.6		
Integrated coal-gasification combined cycle (IGCC)	85	76.1	6.9	31.7	1.2	115.9		
IGCC with CCS	85	97.8	9.8	38.6	1.2	147.4		
Natural Gas-fired								
Conventional combined cycle	87	14.3	1.7	49.1	1.2	66.3		
Advanced combined cycle	87	15.7	2.0	45.5	1.2	64.4		
Advanced CC with CCS	87	30.3	4.2	55.6	1.2	91.3		
Conventional combustion turbine	30	40.2	2.8	82.0	3.4	128.4		
Advanced combustion turbine	30	27.3	2.7	70.3	3.4	103.8		
Advanced nuclear	90	71.4	11.8	11.8	1.1	96.1	−10.0	86.1
Geothermal	92	34.2	12.2	0.0	1.4	47.9	−3.4	44.5
Biomass	83	47.4	14.5	39.5	1.2	102.6		
Non-dispatchable Technologies								
Wind	35	64.1	13.0	0.0	3.2	80.3		
Wind-offshore	37	175.4	22.8	0.0	5.8	204.1		
Solar PV[2]	25	114.5	11.4	0.0	4.1	130		
Solar Thermal	20	195.0	42.1	0.0	6.0	243.1		
Hydro[3]	53	72.0	4.1	6.4	2.0	284.5		

Source Adapted by Author (2014) from US Energy Information Administration (2014a, b) Annual energy outlook 2014

to a degree what energy infrastructure is built and supported through incentives through energy law. For example, in the table below, subsidies are factored in for nuclear energy and geothermal only.

The cost comparisons for energy sources are usually completed by economists. In general, following the leading economic school of thought—the neoclassical economic school—there is a focus on the return on investment in the short to medium term. This does not favour an energy source like nuclear energy where the initial fixed costs (construction) are high but the variable costs (fuel and operation) are low. This is in contrast to many other energy sources and in particular fossil fuels where the fixed cost is low but the variable costs are high (and also unstable as they fluctuate quite significantly).

As yet, controlling pollution from all energy sources is still a technical and policy challenge. It is only in the past 10–15 years that coal plants have had more environmental restrictions placed on them. In both the US and EU this has seen a significant decrease in the number of new coal plants constructed—there is more on this in Chap. 3.

2.2.6 Energy Law for Energy Waste Management

Energy law for waste management in the energy sector is probably one of the most controversial areas in energy law. For example, the waste from nuclear energy sector is a popular issue in society and often used as a key reason as to why there is limited support for nuclear energy infrastructure development in some countries.

Nuclear waste management is a complex issue and there are different types of nuclear energy waste. The disposal of high-level nuclear waste is an issue and several countries are building long-term underground storage facilities; other countries are also planning this. There are also problems with waste from other energy sources. These perhaps do not receive as much publicity, yet they are also harmful; and in many cases the legislation is not as clear as that for the nuclear energy sector. In particular, fossil fuel energy sources produce CO_2, which is a form of energy waste and as yet no solution has been implemented to solve this waste issue; the introduction of a carbon tax has had very limited success where applied. Carbon capture storage (CCS) technology is aimed at reducing the waste from fossil fuel plants, by capturing CO_2 emissions from fossil fuel plants in three stages: capture, transport and storage. There are also other waste issues from fossil fuels, including offshore oil and gas rigs, and old coalmines.

In contrast, the low-carbon energy sector produces less waste. Nuclear energy waste has been detailed above but nuclear energy produces a limited amount of CO_2. Renewable energy sources generate a limited amount of waste, however, they do have shorter lifespans, usually of 25 years maximum, so this relatively short (in the context of energy plants) lifespan of the infrastructure does mean more waste.

The energy waste management policy of a country is generally seen as separate to energy policy and in many cases taken out of the energy cycle in policy terms. In general, different energy law applies to it, and it may not be contained in the main energy legislation. The management of energy waste is a growing business sector, however, energy waste management has high fixed (set-up) costs and this leads to slower growth in the sector. In addition, there is an issue with the public's reluctance to live near energy waste facilities. However, new policies are expected in many countries, certainly across Europe, and in particular for nuclear energy waste management. The same is not happening for other energy sources. The nuclear energy industry is engaging with the public too, and recently in the UK there was an announcement that those areas that are willing to consider the establishment of a nuclear waste management facility in their town will receive up to £40 million (The Guardian 2014).

2.2.7 Connection to Local Energy Law

National energy law is the major driver of where energy infrastructure is located and as a result affects local energy law. At local level, there is significant local energy law that directly affects the public living near energy infrastructure. There is also scope for further financial incentives at a local level for energy infrastructure developers and operators. National energy law may permit a degree of autonomy to local districts to assist them in encouraging energy infrastructure development in their districts. The attraction of employment opportunities arising from the construction and then continued operation of the energy plant can be of significant value for local districts.

2.2.8 Final Reflections

> *Understand and consider the following*:
>
> - **What is the difference between international and national energy law?**
> - **Examine the energy legislation of a country of your choice**
> - **What is national energy law? Give an example of one that is affected by international energy law**

2.3 Local Energy Law

2.3.1 Local Competing Demands

In a similar way to international and national energy law, local energy law faces the three determinants of the energy law and policy triangle (see Fig. 1.1). At a local level, the public is more directly affected by new energy infrastructure. The economic benefits of such a project are significant and are viewed as leading to an increase in local employment. For example, a nuclear energy project can see the creation of around 25,000 employment opportunities over the course of a decade and nearly 900 jobs at the site itself for its lifetime (60 years) for ongoing operations (EDF 2014).

Environmental concerns are a major issue. First, the public plays a key role in the planning process. Energy infrastructure developers have to ensure that they accommodate the local community and deal with their concerns. This is increasingly important in order to avoid issues being raised when construction is already ongoing and before operation begins. Project delays can be extremely costly at this planning phase, and the more practical solution for the developer is to ensure that all problems have reached a resolution from the outset of this phase. Environmental concerns can include potential air pollution, water pollution, views of the landscape and post-accident emergency plans.

The public also now has more of a voice due to Environmental Impact Assessments (EIAs) and the Aarhus Convention being applied in most countries. An EIA is intended by international and national communities to achieve a balance between development and the environment. It is a vehicle for stakeholder consultation and participation. EIA legislation was introduced in the US over 40 years ago and in the EU in 1985; 140 countries worldwide now have some sort of EIA system. The EIA system is now supported by the Aarhus Convention which aims to secure a democratic right of participation in environmental issues; this is explained in more detail at Sect. 2.3.5.

Local politics also plays a role in the development of local energy law. Local politicians have a more direct relationship with the public than national politicians. Economic and environmental issues are of great importance to the public and therefore to local politicians. The latter have to address the public's concerns as well as ensure compliance with their national political party aims. Local politicians play a major role in determining the delivery of benefits from an energy infrastructure project and ensuring the developers of such a project also receive benefits for developing the project in their district.

2.3.2 *Infrastructure Location*

The main question for local energy law formulation is where the energy infrastructure will be located. Oil, gas and nuclear infrastructure have a history now with certain local communities. These communities are generally receptive to the increased development of energy infrastructure. They have experienced the benefits and want them to continue. This is the reason why there exist clusters of energy infrastructure in many countries. An example of this is the new UK nuclear build programme. All the reactors are being built on or near existing nuclear energy infrastructure—Hinkley Point, Sizewell, Wylfa Newydd, Oldbury and Moorside.

For other energy infrastructure, establishing a relationship with local communities is a vital step. Wind farms, hydroelectric dams, solar farms, coal-bed methane, and unconventional oil and gas onshore drilling face a significant hurdle in developing the relevant infrastructure. Local communities have to be receptive to change and the adoption of new local energy law is essential. In some cases, the necessary energy law emanates from national energy law, but in others there are changes to local planning, environmental, employment and finance law.

2.3.3 Introduction of Other Legal Issues and Development of Local Energy Law

Local energy law is perhaps not specifically stated as energy law at the moment. Currently local energy law arises from other areas of the law such as planning law, environmental law, local government legislation and revenue/tax law. Local energy law will develop into its own area as local energy infrastructure increases and it will be formed by specific issues such as the following: planning appeals; grid connection issues; community development issues; land and property ownership issues; investment, option and bank finance agreements; liability issues; and health and safety issues (including emergency preparedness procedures).

Changes will also be specific to the attributes of the local area and the local population, and depend on what energy infrastructure is planned. Businesses may receive lower tax rates (in some form), and planning regulations may require 'offset' measures that mean the design of the energy infrastructure fits in with the location, and the limits outlined by environmental law measures relating to pollution and conservation that are imposed upon the energy infrastructure developer.

While these actions happen separately at the moment in many countries, it will be the case in future that local districts develop a more holistic approach (as outlined in the first paragraph of this sub-section). Having their own specific energy law will allow more transparency in the process of how energy infrastructure is built.

2.3.4 Local Actors: Who Has the Key Influence?

From the previous sections (Sects. 2.3.1–2.3.3) it can be determined that local government has a key role in formulating local energy law such as for example, the local planning authority and environmental agency. In many cases these are divisions or agents of local government. There is also the regional or local development agency and their responsibilities will include deciding on potential benefits that an energy infrastructure developer will receive. These may include benefits per person employed, land use incentives and other development aid. It is important to note that these benefits are not exclusive to the energy sector but available to all businesses.

There are two other key actors in relation to local energy sector development and these are non-public-sector related. The first of these is energy companies, which naturally play a significant role as the project developers and/or energy plant operators. Energy companies have a number of functions at the local level. They decide on what benefits to give the local community, ensure their project plans are transparent and available to the public, and, more indirectly, have some level of interaction (influence) with local politicians.

The second of these non-public-sector actors is the public itself, perhaps in the form of local civil rights groups. Usually these are in the form of environmental groups. These groups participate in the planning process for the new energy infrastructure. They may be concerned about a long list of issues that depend in part upon the particular area where the energy infrastructure is located. Issues may include conservation (nature and wildlife), impact on tourism, destruction of scenery (views), air and water pollution, volume of traffic and impact upon local services (hospitals, schools and transport). Environmental groups can have a strong influence especially if they have links with national environmental groups. Planning applications can be delayed from normal one- to two-year processes to five- or six-year processes in some cases. With delays in the planning process being quite costly, it is important that energy companies engage directly with local environmental and civil rights groups.

2.3.5 *The Aarhus Convention*

There is a democratic right of participation in environmental issues under the Aarhus Convention. The Aarhus Convention is the name given to the UN Economic Commission for Europe's Convention on Access to Information, Participation in Decision-making and Access to Justice in Environmental Matters established in 1998. It has 46 signatories and however was only ratified in 2009 and entered into force then when 16 signatories in total had ratified it. The Aarhus Convention grants the public rights regarding access to information, public participation and access to justice, in governmental decision-making processes on matters concerning the local, national and transboundary environment. It focuses on interactions between the public and the public authorities.

The Aarhus Convention is a part of international energy law but it has a local effect. It perhaps has more relevance to developed countries as it is usually provided for within the Environmental Impact Assessment (EIA) process of developed countries. However, the Convention may have limited application due to local political and business interest issues but in theory it is present and its application is improving in developed countries and even in many developing countries. It raises the question of Corporate Social Responsibility for energy companies. Do international energy companies behave responsibly at a local level in less developed countries? Do they go through the same steps as their project develops that they would go through in a developed country or their own home county? This is an area for critical reflection for students as it an under-researched area and one on which there is no 'right' conclusion.

2.3.6 Energy Infrastructure: New Build Practice

Previous sections have been normative and concern what should happen. However, what is expected to happen often does not necessarily do so. In energy law, a student needs to research what the law states and what actually happens in practice.

In general, new build practice for energy infrastructure involves the following:

- build on existing site or build near/adjacent to other energy infrastructure;
- build in areas where region dependent on this type of employment;
- utilise expertise available locally (from existing energy plants); and
- utilise existing education of the local population to engage quickly and agree on any issues with the local community.

The process is very difficult if new energy infrastructure is built on a new site and/or a new area/region. Energy companies will want to avoid this as they will have to interact with a new community and will not benefit from the pre-existing structures in the local community and local government that they would have when building on or adjacent to an existing site. The costs of satisfying a local community can be high but even more expensive can be delays to the project and the resulting interest accrued on project finance.

2.3.7 Connection to Energy Policy Concepts

In considering international, national and local energy law it is necessary to understand key energy policies that directly affect the formulation of law at each level. For example, electricity policy can have a major influence at local level due to the level of access to the electricity grid and the management of the electricity network. It is for this reason that local energy law will become more important and more developed over time as there are developments in the deployment of more localised energy production and more access is made to the electricity grid. In addition, the benefit of building where an existing energy plant cluster exists already is that there will also be access to the electricity grid. Building on new sites may require the energy company to contribute to the development of electricity grid access. For some projects this cost may be an insurmountable obstacle to its approval by investors.

2.3.8 Final Reflections

Understand and consider the following:

- **What is the power of local energy law?**
- **Other legal subjects are relevant to local energy law—what are they and why are they relevant?**
- **What is an EIA?**

2.4 Recommended Reading

These are the main journals in the area of energy law; then there are subject-specific journals, and finally more general energy journals where there will be articles from numerous disciplines.

Energy Law Journals

1. Energy Law Journal
2. European Energy and Environmental Law Review
3. European Energy Journal
4. International Energy Law Review
5. Journal of Energy and Natural Resources Law (IBA)
6. Journal of World Energy Law and Business
7. Natural Resources Journal
8. Oil, Gas and Energy Law
9. San Diego Journal of Climate and Energy Law
10. The Texas Journal of Oil, Gas and Energy Law

Energy Source Specific Law and Policy Journals
Some of these journals also publish scientific articles

11. A Journal of Renewable Energy Law and Policy
12. Annals of Nuclear Energy
13. International Journal of Nuclear Law
14. International Shale Gas and Oil Journal
15. Journal of Unconventional Oil and Gas Resources
16. LSU Journal of Energy Law and Resources
17. Nuclear Law Bulletin
18. Oil and Gas Journal
19. Progress in Nuclear Energy
20. Renewable Energy Strategy Reviews

General Energy Related Journals

21. Applied Energy
22. Energy
23. Energy Economics
24. Energy Policy
25. Energy Procedia
26. Energy Strategy Reviews
27. Harvard Environmental Law Review
28. Nature
29. Nature Climate Change
30. Science

References

Burgherr P, Hirschberg S (2014) Comparative risk assessment of severe accidents in the energy sector. Energy Policy. doi: 10.1016/j.enpol.2014.01.035

Department of Energy and Climate Change (DECC) (2014) UK energy statistics, 27 March 2014. https://www.gov.uk/government/uploads/system/uploads/attachment_data/file/296183/pn_march_14.pdf. Accessed 18 Oct 2014

EDF (2014) Hinkley point C—an opportunity to power the future. http://www.edfenergy.com/energy/nuclear-new-build-projects/hinkley-point-c. Accessed 18 Oct 2014

Environmental Protection Agency (EPA) (2014) Fuel mix for US electricity generation. http://www.epa.gov/cleanenergy/energy-and-you/. Accessed 18 Oct 2014

The Guardian (Carrington, D) (2014) Communities could be paid £40 for considering nuclear waste dump, Thursday 24 July 2014. http://www.theguardian.com/environment/2014/jul/24/communities-could-be-paid-40m-for-considering-nuclear-waste-dump. Accessed 18 Oct 2014

US Energy Information Administration (EIA) (2014a) Annual energy outlook 2014, 30 April 2014, DOE/EIA-0383 (2014). http://www.eia.gov/forecasts/aeo/electricity_generation.cfm. Accessed 18 Oct 2014

US Energy Information Administration (EIA) (2014b) China. http://www.eia.gov/countries/cab.cfm?fips=ch. Accessed 18 Oct 2014

Chapter 3
Issues in Energy Law

3.1 Energy Policy Concepts

3.1.1 Electricity Policy

Electricity policy forms the key part of energy policy. Often when the term 'energy policy' is used, the electricity sector is being referred to. The inputs and outputs of the energy sector concern mainly electricity production. However, the energy sector is also concerned with energy use in the transport, industrial, property and agricultural sectors. This book views energy policy as being connected in some degree to electricity policy.

Electricity policy centres around the electricity market at first instance. The electricity market where electricity is sold is either regulated or deregulated. These are economic terms, and in their simplest forms a regulated market is one where prices are fixed and a deregulated market is one where prices are not fixed and are left to the market to achieve a competitive price.

The electricity regulator plays an important role in the electricity sector. It ensures that in a regulated market, prices are not set too high, and that in a deregulated market, prices are fair and do not inhibit either consumers or producers. The electricity regulator will usually decide the electricity market formation. Its objective is usually to have a fair electricity price and also a market where new energy infrastructure is encouraged along with the advances in technology that will increase efficiency of energy production and use. Advances in technology come from innovation, and research and development, which a good electricity policy would encourage. Achieving these aims is difficult and many countries struggle.

This issue is an important one for students to consider. The question arises, is the electricity price fair given the average income in society and the profits (or losses) that energy companies earn?

Part of Sect. 3.1.2 is from an article entitled: Heffron (2012). And part of Sect. 3.1.11 is from an article entitled: Heffron (2013). Thanks are expressed to the publishers of these journals.

© The Author(s) 2015
R.J. Heffron, *Energy Law: An Introduction*,
SpringerBriefs in Law, DOI 10.1007/978-3-319-14191-6_3

3.1.2 Competition Policy and Energy Sources

Competition policy is of relevance for those countries with deregulated electricity markets. In general there will be rules to competition set out by the electricity regulator. This is to ensure a fair, transparent and competitive electricity market structure for energy companies. There are two main aims of competition policy with the first being to enhance economic efficiency, and the second being to limit market power, i.e. monopolies. Adam Smith was one of the first to state that competition could be thwarted by 'the great engine of [...] monopoly' (Smith 1776, Book 1, Chap. 10, para IV.7.175). His view was that excessive market power may lead the market mechanism to fail to allocate scarce resources as efficiently as it otherwise could. He stated that 'People of the same trade seldom meet together, even for merriment and diversion, but the conservation ends in conspiracy against the public, or in some contrivance to raise prices' (Smith 1776, Book 1, Chap. 10, para I.10.82). It is in this context that competition law seeks to determine the appropriate mix between competition and cooperation in the economy by identifying the legal parameters for cooperative activity.

Competition policy is one of the main goals of the European Union. It aims to harmonise product markets across the EU. The success of this policy is open to question. It has worked for some products but not for others. In particular, the view from research is that competitive markets do not work for products that are considered 'public goods'—which are goods that increase the well-being of society and are provided by government or the private sector for no profit. The question of whether electricity is a public good is open to question but increasingly it is seen as one. Energy poverty has become a key social issue and one that is likely to increase in its political importance for many countries.

In the UK, the push for competition has resulted in less competition in the electricity sector. The energy sector was privatised by the Conservative government nearly 20 years ago. However, despite the intention of this policy, competition has decreased, with the number of electricity and gas suppliers falling from around 20 in the early 1990s to only six: British Gas, EDF, E.on, Npower, Scottish Power, and Scottish and Southern Electric. These six companies supply around 99 % of homes in the UK. The electricity and gas sector is an oligopoly and customers have seen a gradual rise in their prices despite the initial price decrease after privatisation. To further compound matters, investment in new generation by the incumbents has been poor and, new investment is needed for new generation facilities with the investment estimates ranging from £100 billion to £200 billion. Clearly competition needs to be reviewed in the sector, which is not delivering on price for consumers in the short term, or the long term when the failure to invest in new generation is factored in.

For a student the questions arise as to whether competition is a notional concept in the electricity sector, and why is this maybe so? In addition, there is the question that emanates from the energy law and policy triangle: is competition achievable for a country that also wants to reduce CO_2 emissions and increase its energy security?

3.1.3 Energy Waste Management Policy

Each country has its own energy waste management policy. To date there is limited international law on this issue for the energy sector except in the nuclear energy industry. There are firm international commitments in the nuclear energy sector to recycling some nuclear waste and to developing a solution for the long-term storage of other nuclear waste. However, there are still no clear solutions for the nuclear energy sector, although in the EU all Member States must have a new policy and law in place for nuclear energy waste by 2015 and notify the European Commission of this plan (Council Directive 2011/70/Euratom).

For many other energy sources the issue of energy waste management has not yet been resolved. For example, the estimated cost of decommissioning old oil and gas rigs in the North Sea, off the coast of Scotland, was estimated at £30 billion— for which the oil and gas industry will receive tax relief (Burges Salmon 2013). An effort has been made in relation to carbon capture storage (CCS) technology to find an EU solution rather than a national solution; however, Canada, the US and China remain the leaders in developing and conducting research in CCS projects.

For a student an interesting project is to examine waste management policy in a number of countries and for a number of energy sources. A student can obtain a limited but useful amount of information in the *Yearbook for International Environmental Law*, published by Oxford University Press and produced annually with country reports.

'Good' energy law should aspire to also incorporate an energy waste management policy. In some cases it does so, in that energy producers are required by legislation to contribute to an energy waste management plan; however, it is usually limited to this action alone. This needs to become a factor in decisions on which energy infrastructure to build.

3.1.4 Planning Policy

Planning law plays a key role in energy law and policy formation as stated earlier in Chaps. 1 and 2. Planning policy is generally decided at national level and with a certain level of local autonomy as long as it aligns with national considerations.

In many countries planning law for large infrastructure projects that are of national significance means they can be fast-tracked through the planning process. The UK's planning policy even specifically mentions energy infrastructure projects as an example of such nationally significant infrastructure projects. Other policy issues (as mentioned in Sect. 2.3) concern the location of energy infrastructure; the connection to the electricity grid; building on new or old 'sites'; and environmental concerns near construction sites.

There are efforts to harmonise planning law across Europe by the EU. These emanate from the development of energy infrastructure and in particular electricity grid infrastructure such as grid connectors. The difficulty is that these grid connectors will play an important role in having a single electricity market across Europe but at the moment their construction is proving difficult since different countries have different planning laws. Cross-border infrastructure development therefore becomes more complex. The EU in 2013 made €5.85 billion available for such projects (through the Connecting Europe Facility) (European Commission 2014), and is also developing its plans for harmonising planning law for cross-border energy projects in the EU under the TransEuropean Networks for Energy (TEN-E) Regulations (EU Regulation 347/2013 on TEN-E).

3.1.5 Energy Security

Energy security is increasingly an issue for many countries. There are very few international countries which are 100 % energy independent. In the past energy security was not such a concern for many countries because energy prices were reasonable and mostly stable. However, over the past decade energy prices have begun to fluctuate more and have become increasingly expensive. The result has placed financial pressure on many countries for two reasons, the first being high prices and the second being fluctuating prices which mean that countries cannot accurately calculate national budgets; this contributes to economic uncertainty.

For politicians this has become a key issue. High international energy prices are passed on to consumers and generally energy prices never return to their former level even if in international markets they fall—this is particularly the case in the UK, which has in part led to a new Office of Gas and Electricity Markets (OFGEM) investigation into energy companies. Politicians are increasingly worried about the effect of high energy prices and how they may influence election outcomes. If one such energy price crisis occurs (or even if there are electricity blackouts) at election time then the likelihood is that the incumbent politicians will be voted out. This has imposed extra pressure on politicians to secure some level of energy security. This may be part of the reason why national governments in many countries are allowing wide-scale shale gas exploration and extraction despite it not being subject to the same health, safety and environmental regulations as other existing energy sources.

Energy security will only become more important. With the attempts by the EU to form one single electricity market, many governments have been prompted to see energy exports as a potential revenue stream and this policy is being adopted by many countries. Also in the EU, the over-reliance on Russian gas is set to change policy. With political relations with Russia deteriorating due to the Crimea and Ukraine situations, the EU is beginning to look at alternatives to Russian gas. In particular many Eastern European states are vulnerable; however, many of these states have had as part of their own energy policies for some time the aim of reducing their reliance on Russian energy.

Energy security is a key EU energy policy goal at the moment, and in many states across the world the ambition is similar. Energy prices have become too volatile, and a question for students is why? Is it due to a lack of competition or regulation in financial markets, or does the problem lie in the market structure? With the ongoing financial downturn in economies worldwide, politicians place significant importance on maintaining stability and public confidence in the economy, and greater energy security is one element in ensuring this increased economic stability.

3.1.6 National Energy Policy

National energy policy and its formulation are similar to what was stated in Sect. 2.2. This section simply aims to re-emphasise the point that national energy policy changes with different governments. The degree to which it changes can be different. Australia recently had a significant change in its energy policy with a new prime minister in 2013 and went from a low-carbon orientation back to fossil fuel—more detail is give in Chap. 4. Canada also had a change in energy policy with a change of government in 2006, and no longer has a low-carbon economy as a major goal of energy policy, as it had prior to 2006—more detail is give in Chap. 4. Too often governments view the energy sector with a short-term perspective and this inhibits investment in and deployment of low-carbon energy technology.

In some countries energy policy has always been viewed with a long-term perspective. The energy policy of Denmark over the past 40–50 years is an example of long-term ambition and achievement (Ronne 2013). Denmark, through the energy law and policy followed and developed by successive governments, has changed from a country that relied 100 % on imports to one that has 100 % its own production, and now is 40 % of the way to 100 % carbon-free energy production. Denmark exemplifies the impact and significance that energy law can have, and the reason why a country would choose to have independent energy legislation.

In France, during the 1970s and 1980s energy policy was in essence predetermined without the periodic influence of politics. This led to its successful nuclear energy programme, which resulted in France having a low-carbon electricity system. Perhaps the lesson is that politicians need to engage with each other on energy policy and agree on energy policy irrespective of which political party in government. Considering the volatility in energy prices, such cooperation could be considered strategic for politicians.

3.1.7 International Energy Policy

International energy policy has in some respects been examined in Sect. 2.1.1. However, in this review of energy policy concepts, it is important to highlight international energy policy. Different international organisations have different agendas and engage in what is referred to as 'agenda-setting'.

In many cases it is international organisations with member countries that engage in this activity, such as the World Bank and the UN. However, there are other entities that try and engage in 'agenda-setting'. In particular, these can be seen in relation to climate change. The influence of multinational companies should not be ignored here. There are 90 entities (mostly companies) that are responsible for two thirds of CO_2 emissions in the world (Heede 2014). It should be noted that these companies do engage in varying degrees of political, economic and social policy lobbying. Nowhere is this more evident than in the US where climate change counter-movement lobbying firms (including think tanks) received just over $900 million in annual income (Brulle 2014)—or perhaps in the US the data is just more transparent. Nevertheless the influence of these corporations is outlined by Hertz (2001) in her book *The Silent Takeover* where she emphasises the reach that global corporations can have on society.

3.1.8 Heritage Policy

New energy infrastructure can affect the heritage of a country. There are many cases where infrastructure projects have destroyed heritage sites. This is part of the reason why there is now a global heritage regime, one of the bigger successes of the UN. Heritage sites can now be classed as UN-recognised World Heritage Sites, and this means certain regulations of protection and preservation are applied to the site.

Often the infrastructure that infringes upon heritage sites is energy infrastructure. This is perhaps most common in the Middle East recently where many hydro-electric power dams have been built. These have been at the expense of heritage sites which have been submerged in water. Turkey is an example here, and in particular one can look there at the heritage site which has been submerged in the city of Hasankeyf.

There is, however, a realisation that protecting the heritage of one's nation is important for the tourism industry. There is an increasing reluctance to damage heritage for new infrastructure, including energy infrastructure. Specifically, this can be seen in the UK, where wind farms can affect the view from heritage sites and this is not seen as attractive. In essence, heritage law and policy has to compete with energy law and policy concerning the location of the energy infrastructure. Many countries do find it difficult to balance the aims of each but now aim to protect heritage. However, other countries still favour the energy industry. One recent example of this is the development of a coal ship route over the Great Barrier Reef in Australia. The Great Barrier Reef is a UNESCO World Heritage Site and yet this development is still happening. The Great Barrier Reef attracts $3 billion (Australian dollars) in tourism and is one of the world's largest coral reef systems (Australian Government: Great Barrier Reef Marine Park Authority 2005). Yet the continued development of the energy sector is deemed more important.

3.1.9 Environmental Policy

Environmental policy issues have been covered in brief in Chap. 2, and one of the key issues was where the energy infrastructure is located. Other issues concerned where will access to the electricity grid be, and what the local environmental concerns will be, such as effects to local wildlife, water, CO_2 emissions etc. The reader should recap earlier arguments as this discussion flows from that too.

One of the major questions of environmental policy in relation to energy law and policy is, can national environmental concerns outweigh local environmental concerns? An example of the logic behind the argument here is that if a country wants to reduce its national CO_2 emissions and build new energy infrastructure, can some local environmental concerns be bypassed or essentially not taken into account? These local concerns will be a cost of the new energy infrastructure with the latter ultimately leading to a better environment nationally and internationally (in terms of CO_2 emissions).

A review of legislation in the area suggests that energy infrastructure that is of national importance can supersede local environmental concerns. For example, a key provision of the UK Planning Act 2008 was the introduction of a new system for approving major infrastructure projects of national importance. The objective was to streamline these decisions and avoid long public inquiries (with an estimated saving of £300 million a year). The hearing and decision-making processes are rigidly bound to a timetable. The Act even specifically states that the system will be used for energy developments such as large-scale renewable projects, and for nuclear power. Nevertheless, local actors increasingly have a stronger voice than before, and the aforementioned Aarhus Convention (see Sect. 2.3.1) gives the public a stronger voice. Its application over the next decade will be interesting to follow. This is also an area for the reader interested in the overlap of energy and environmental law, which is covered in Sect. 3.1.11.

3.1.10 Importance of Energy Policy Concepts

For the student in energy law and policy, it important to know about the energy policy concepts as these can all contribute to the formulation of energy law. Different political parties place different emphasis on these concepts and consequently energy law and policy may be formulated that is vastly different to that of the previous political party in government. For example, consider the Australian Labor political party in 2012 with an energy policy to develop a carbon pricing mechanism at its core. Then after a change of leadership in the political party, the government immediately repealed this legislation and announced major investments in the fossil fuel industry, thus disembarking Australia from its previous path towards being a low-carbon economy.

A student needs to know the differences and similarities of different energy concepts and their potential outcomes in general and in specific countries. Different countries have different priorities. In the example above, Australia, has turned to developing economic benefits from exporting fossil fuels while other policy concepts (such as the environment) are not given priority.

3.1.11 The Relationship Between Energy and Environmental Law

From an international perspective, energy law is emerging at a fast pace in legal practice and in the academic literature. Increasingly, energy issues are featuring prominently in national political and industrial discourse. In particular, energy issues have been pushed higher up on the agenda with the advent of climate change and policies concerning energy security. Politicians can be credited with pushing the agenda, in part, because electricity prices have a major influence on election outcomes. However, there is also the realisation that the energy sector can play an important role in the economy in terms of economic growth and job creation.

There needs to be more ambition in the formulation of energy law and it should be viewed as a distinct field in the promotion and evolution of sustainable economic development. Energy law through 'targeted legislation' can ensure that a nation moves towards a low-carbon economy and it can directly contribute to mitigating the effects of climate change. Further, energy legislation can aid and encourage new investment in the energy sector. In this context, for many countries, environmental law can no longer manage energy sources effectively; distinct new energy law is needed for long-term sustainability, climate change mitigation and environmental protection.

The Similar Characteristics of Energy and Environmental Law
Energy law and environmental law have similar characteristics. Both are concerned with legislating for the effective management of natural resources. However, in the case of energy law, the natural resources with which it is concerned are those that can yield energy directly, or possess the potential to do so, and thereby contribute to electricity production. Hence, major concerns of environmental law, such as forestry, habitat and wildlife are not a focus of energy law. Nevertheless, the link between them is obvious given the potential of energy assets to threaten forestry, habitat or wildlife by its location or as a result of its pollution.

Both energy law and environmental law share the characteristic of aiming to change behaviour. This is significant in that both have as a main aim to contribute to climate change mitigation. The effectiveness therefore of energy and environmental law is paramount in mitigating the effects of climate change. In the case of EU countries there are also the climate change obligations they have to meet under the EU 2020 targets (European Commission 2007). These targets are to ensure not just better human health from good air quality but also the health and well-being of future generations.

The importance of energy law and environmental law is in providing legislation to manage the natural resources of a country and their potential for changing human and societal behaviour; another important characteristic is that of policy formulation. Both energy and environmental law demonstrate to a greater capacity than other areas of the law the interchange between law and policy, and the importance of policy-makers. Policy development drives forward energy and environmental law. Environmental law has at its core an international agenda that informs and pushes regions to implement the various international treaties and consequently to legislate for these. Energy law is affected by national energy policy, which in turn is driven by international agreements or targets, for example, the aforementioned EU 2020 climate change targets. In this merging of law and policy, lawyers through their understanding of law can play a key role in ensuring that effective policy is created, thus facilitating the development of effective law.

3.1.12 Final Reflection

Understand and consider the following:

- **Know the key energy policy concepts**
- **Be able to discuss distinct features of the electricity market in your country**
- **Compare the main rules of the electricity market in one country with another country**
- **Energy law is old but has returned in prominence—why?**
- **Does energy law follow environmental law? Which follows which?**
- **Understand that energy law and climate change are increasingly interconnected**

3.2 Law for Fossil Fuels

3.2.1 Introduction

There are different energy sources and while some energy law is applicable to them all, there is also a distinct amount of energy law specific to different energy sources. If energy sources are considered in terms of a lifecycle of extraction, operation and waste treatment, it is generally at the operation level that there will be similar legislation. Further, within this operation, it is mainly just electricity legislation and regulation that will apply to all energy sources.

The law for different energy sources can be considered under four main categories which are: (1) environment and waste; (2) planning; (3) financial support schemes; and (4) safety issues. Each energy source will be considered in relation to these four characteristics in the sub-sections below.

3.2.2 Gas and Shale Gas

Gas as an energy source plays a dominant role in the energy mix of many countries whether they own their own gas supplies or import it. Gas drilling occurs both onshore and offshore and, along with the operation of gas-fired electricity generation plants, involves a range of different issues—see Table 3.1.

Gas is a fossil fuel energy source and would be affected by a carbon tax though not to the same degree as coal or oil. Gas produces less carbon than coal or oil, and in many countries it is seen as a transitional solution whereby it replaces coal as an energy source and therefore reduces CO_2 emissions. Gas, despite a long history of extraction and use for electricity production, still receives a significant amount of subsidies at the extraction phase—through the form of tax relief. Safety is definitely a concern in the extraction phase and there have been a number of major accidents in gas drilling and plant operation activities. The data on accidents in the gas sector shows that the accident rate is above average for energy sources—see Table 2.3.

A new development is 'fracking' for shale gas, and this is seen as a contentious issue in many countries and a major opportunity in others. Shale gas projects are relatively new and the research into their environmental effects are not yet sufficient, with the law being very reactive towards shale gas rather than proactive. Legislation needs to be updated to some degree to meet safety and environmental

Table 3.1 Gas characteristics

Category	Environment and waste	Planning law	Finance	Safety
Is there a key issue?	Yes	Yes	Yes	Yes
Key issue	Produces CO_2 Flaring Old exploration rigs Chemical use (fracking)	In many cases now, there is significant local opposition to living near 'fracking' operations—i.e. drilling for onshore shale gas	Offshore gas exploration receives a significant amount of subsidies. Shale gas exploration is now also receiving subsidies	Offshore gas exploration has a high amount of accidents. There is not yet sufficient data for shale gas operations

Source Constructed by Author (2014)

concerns. Shale gas, while being heavily extracted in the US, has been banned in France. The UK is struggling to get an operational shale gas sector owing to local stakeholders being against shale gas drilling.

The question arises as to whether the safety legislation in the gas sector is rigorous enough. This is a question for students to explore and answer.

3.2.3 Oil

Oil is also a fossil fuel and has similar characteristics to gas in terms of extraction. Oil is different to the other two fossil fuels (gas and coal) in that oil is used to a limited extent for electricity production but mainly as a fuel in transport and in home heating.

A brief examination in Table 3.2 of the key characteristics of oil that impact on society highlights key problems in the oil sector. Oil produces CO_2 and again its future production will suffer from any introduction of carbon tax legislation. The oil industry also receives many subsidies, mainly for extraction activities and in the form of tax breaks. There are also many safety issues in the oil sector. Again the question arises—similar to that for the gas sector—as to whether the legislation is rigorous enough. An interesting study for a student to complete is a comparison of safety legislation in the oil and gas sectors.

The most recent oil disaster was the BP Deepwater Horizon oil spill accident in the US in 2010. This has followed many accidents in both extraction and transport —see Table 2.3. In many of these accidents there have been fatalities, and with many oil spills there has been significant environmental damage. The total costs for the BP Deepwater Horizon accident have not yet been finalised but are estimated to exceed \$40 billion.

The BP Deepwater Horizon accident case demonstrates several issues. There is new technology and its application needs new business and safety practices. The issue is whether there is sufficient legislation or regulation of these activities, and again in many cases legislation is not being proactive enough in terms of following developments within the sector.

Table 3.2 Oil characteristics

Category	Environment and waste	Planning law	Finance	Safety
Is there a key issue?	Yes	Yes	Yes	Yes
Key issue	Produces CO_2	In some cases there is a difference between underground and overground property rights for shale gas	Receives a significant amount of subsidies for offshore exploration activities	The oil sector has a high number of accidents. Is there a need for reform of safety legislation?

Source Constructed by Author (2014)

3.2.4 Coal

Coal has been the dominant energy source in the modern world since the 1800s. Legislation on the coal sector has existed in some form in many countries since then. It is only in the past 50 years that society has moved to reduce coal burning. This is mainly because there are visible effects of burning coal and these have occurred in many highly densely populated cities in the form of smog. Some of the key characteristics of coal are shown in Table 3.3.

Coal extraction and coal use has had many economic and social effects on society. It contributed to early economic development in the 1800s and early 1900s. However, in terms of the environment, it produces CO_2 and also many other toxic pollutants. The desire for new coal plants has reduced in many developed countries such as the US (through the Clean Air Act 1990) and in the EU. In the EU, limits were placed on new coal production as the EU accepted a new wave of entrants and expanded in 2002–2005 (with the addition of 12 new Member States). In developing countries, coal is still a major source of energy generation. However, China is recognising the effects of coal use on public health in city populations and the resultant cost to the public health services. It is developing new low-carbon energy infrastructure but also considering reducing its reliance on the use of coal in a significant way (expect more developments on this over the next few years).

In many countries there is still substantial support for the coal sector. Many developed countries still rely heavily on coal. For example, there is still a significant amount of coal-fired generation producing electricity in the UK and US with it contributing 36.3 and 39 % of their electricity mix respectively (see Table 2.5). Certainly in the UK there is limited discussion of how to decrease coal use—its use has remained constant for some time. Coal still receives significant subsidies internationally (see Table 3.6).

Safety is a major concern in the coal sector and it has the highest number of fatal accidents as an energy source—see Table 2.3. Whilst a Hollywood movie was made about 33 Chilean miners who were trapped down a mine for 69 days in 2010,

Table 3.3 Coal characteristics

Category	Environment and waste	Planning law	Finance	Safety
Is there a key issue?	Yes	Yes	Yes	Yes
Key issue	Produces CO_2 and several other harmful environmental pollutants	In many cases now there is significant local opposition to living near a coal-fired electricity plant	Receives a significant amount of subsidies mainly now in the developing world but also still in coal mining in the developed world	The coal sector has a high amount of accidents. There is a need for global reform of safety legislation

Source Constructed by Author (2014)

little was said about the accident the following month in the Pike River mine in New Zealand where 29 people died. In general there is specific health and safety legislation for the coal sector; however, enforcement of this legislation and the legislation itself are weak. There continues to be a very high number of fatalities in the coal sector every year, and in particular in China, and this is something to be examined at national and international levels.

3.2.5 Final Reflections

Understand and consider the following:

- **Compare and contrast different countries and their law and policy for fossil fuel energy sources?**

3.3 Law for Low-Carbon Energy Sources

3.3.1 Wind

Wind energy has existed for over a century but has increased in commercial use significantly since the 1970s. The wind energy sector is generally governed by the legislation of the electricity sector. Wind turbines are not a complex infrastructure, unlike many other energy sources. As a result, there are limited issues in terms of safety. Of particular concern to the wind energy sector are the planning issues and finance issues—see Table 3.4.

Table 3.4 Wind characteristics

Category	Environment and waste	Planning law	Finance	Safety
Is there a key issue?	Limited	Yes	Yes	No
Key issue	Produces no CO_2 but can affect the local landscape and wildlife	There are limits as to how many onshore wind turbines can be built on one site and how near to local residents' homes they should be	The wind energy sector is currently in receipt of many subsidies but they are not significant in comparison to fossil fuel subsidies (see Table 3.6)	Not complex technology

Source Constructed by Author (2014)

There is increasingly significant opposition to wind energy at a local level. This has resulted in many wind farm projects being cancelled. However, some countries such as Denmark offer a share in ownership to local residents and towns, though this practice is not widespread. In addition, while wind farms can avail themselves of some financial support through government subsidies, a key issue is the efficiency of the wind turbine and whether it produces enough energy to justify this subsidy. Of course, this can be dependent on who is doing the calculation and what factors they include. For example, wind energy produces no CO_2 and its cost would be lower if a carbon tax was applied. Nevertheless, wind turbines are considered inefficient, but technology is advancing, and some countries such as Denmark have a policy of upgrading their wind turbines to more technologically advanced turbines.

3.3.2 Nuclear Energy

Nuclear energy is a distinctive energy source—key characteristics are presented in Table 3.5. The reason is that it has both a military and a civil use. Nuclear energy has a history of civilian use since after the Second World War. Its military use as a nuclear bomb has impacted upon its civil use. It has created a level of public opposition to nuclear energy that still pervades today. It is a complex technology that is difficult to understand, which contributes to anxiety about its use.

Nuclear energy plants are expensive to build due mainly to having high fixed costs. A significant proportion of the costs occur in their construction phase. When a plant is actually operating, it is very cheap to run, with fuel and operational costs being very low.

Nuclear energy does not produce CO_2 (a limited amount is produced in construction) and each plant produces a significant amount of electricity, so once operational is a good and reliable source of electricity. For nuclear energy the major

Table 3.5 Nuclear energy characteristics

Category	Environment and waste	Planning law	Finance	Safety
Is there a key issue?	Yes	Yes	Yes	No
Key issue	Produces no CO_2 but there is a fuel waste issue	In many cases now there is significant local opposition to living near a nuclear energy plant	Receives some subsidies but not nearly to the same extent as fossil fuel energy sources	There is a big safety culture in the nuclear sector.
				Only three major accidents in the industry worldwide

Source Constructed by Author (2014)

environmental problem is the waste management issue, owing to the fuel used for nuclear energy plants (uranium and plutonium). This nuclear waste has a 'long life' (in the thousands of years) and is currently stored at interim storage repositories usually located at the nuclear plant. Some nuclear waste is recycled but there are only a few of these recycling facilities, and these are in the UK, France, India, Japan and China. Currently the long-term disposal units for nuclear waste are highly developed in Finland and Sweden, with plans to begin development of similar units in many countries (particularly in the EU) over the next few years.

Waste in the nuclear energy sector has to be seen in the context of waste in the energy sector in general. A common argument is that no nuclear energy should be built until a solution is found for its waste issue. This conveniently ignores the waste problem from fossil fuels of CO_2 emissions, not to mention other toxic chemicals that are released from their burning processes.

Nuclear energy is one of the safest energy sources when considered in the context of the energy industry itself—see also Table 2.3. However, if there is an accident, the potential for a major impact is serious, and hence nuclear energy is seen as an energy source with a high risk. There is an established nuclear safety community and regime led by the IAEA, in comparison with other energy sources. There is more developed cooperation among nations in ensuring a global safety regime and practices in the nuclear energy sector. There is a case to be made, however, for nuclear energy legislation to be more proactive; such proactive legislation could have prevented the Fukushima accident (for more on the Fukushima accident, see the recommended reading).

New nuclear energy plans are extensive across the world. Increasingly, they are being built on the same site or next to the sites of existing nuclear energy plants. As stated earlier, this is to overcome potential local opposition at new sites but also to make use of expertise in the local community where the existing nuclear plant is located. The nuclear energy sector receives subsidies but these are not equivalent to the amount that the fossil fuel sector receives.

A global assessment of subsidies in the energy sector (see Table 3.6) demonstrates that fossil fuels receive significant subsidies, circa \$400 billion, though according to the International Energy Agency this figure is unquestionably higher (International Energy Agency 2010). Subsidies for fossil fuels are set to increase too, with them being given now for carbon capture and storage technology development, shale gas and decommissioning in the fossil fuel sector.

Table 3.6 Subsidies to different energy sources

Energy type	Subsidy estimate (US\$ billion/year)
Nuclear energy	45
Renewable energy (excluding hydroelectricity)	27
Biofuels	20
Fossil fuels	400

Source Adapted by Author (2014) from relative subsidies to energy sources. Global Subsidies Initiative (2010)

3.3.3 Hydropower

Hydropower plants have been in commercial operation since the late nineteenth century. The technology involved has developed since then; however, they still can have a significant effect in the region where they are built—see Table 3.7 for more detail.

Hydropower plants produce no CO_2 and are considered one of the more efficient and reliable low-carbon energy sources. They account for circa 15 % of the world's electricity supply. The problem with hydropower is the access to water. This means it is not an energy source for every country, as many will not have sufficient water flows to build one. The environmental impact of a hydropower plant can be significant given its potential to impact on landscape, wildlife, human habitation and heritage sites.

In particular, the impact on humans is a problem. If it is necessary that a town needs to be flooded, this will mean relocation to another location and can increase the cost of the project financially, not to mention the effect on the local community and family lives. Nevertheless, this is a common practice in the Middle East and Asia. In Turkey, several towns and heritage sites have been submerged and people relocated. China, in building the Three Gorges dam, relocated circa 1.2 million and possibly a further 300,000 people (The Guardian 2010).

Hydropower plants generally have available a limited amount of subsidies except where there are significant relocation costs and generally it is not the developer that pays all of these. A further problem with hydropower is its use for international political advantage. This is where there are cross-border water supplies that one country cuts off in order to build its hydropower plants, and as a result the other country suffers from a lack of water or sufficient water levels. In time this may become a issue for many countries in Asia and the Middle East.

Table 3.7 Hydropower characteristics

Category	Environment and waste	Planning law	Finance	Safety
Is there a key issue?	Yes	Yes	Yes	No
Key issue	Produces no CO_2 but has an impact on landscape, wildlife, human habitation, and heritage sites	In some cases yes because of the need to flood towns, and farm lands	Moderate amount but if human relocation taken into account, very high	No real safety issues except for a major accident in China which was due to poor construction and extreme weather from a typhoon (Banqiao Dam 1975)

Source Constructed by Author (2014)

Table 3.8 Solar energy characteristics

Category	Environment and waste	Planning law	Finance	Safety
Is there a key issue?	No	No	Yes	No
Key issue	Few issues here unless a solar farm is near where it can disrupt wildlife habitat	In many cases there are no significant issues	Receives subsidies but not to the same level as fossil fuels	No real issues recorded so far

Source Constructed by Author (2014)

3.3.4 Solar

Solar energy technology has been developing at an increased rate over the last decade. There are now solar farms in many countries and in particular, in the Ukraine, the US, Germany and China.

Solar energy has very few environmental effects and produces no CO_2—see Table 3.8 for more details. The lifespan of solar panels may be an environmental concern. Many manufacturers only offer guarantees for a maximum of 25 years and their performance after this period is an area for future research.

A problem with solar energy is that it is currently expensive, although the costs are set to continue to decrease. In many ways the incentives to deploy solar energy are too low in many countries and they should receive more incentives particularly to accelerate technological development. There are few objections by local communities to solar energy and even in the case of solar farms. Solar energy benefits by being more localised, with individuals seeing the benefit directly, and hence they are less likely to object to any solar energy developments. Solar farms are being developed increasingly in more unusual places such as old airports—and perhaps in time on uninhabitable and over-polluted sites.

3.3.5 Other Low-Carbon Energy Sources

There are other low-energy sources and some of the more technologically advanced of these are wave and tidal energy, biomass, hydrogen, and geothermal—see Table 3.9 for some key issues concerning these. These technologies are not yet been deployed except for biomass and geothermal which are used in a limited way.

Wave and tidal energy can have an impact on the environment below water and is a renewable energy source that is being researched across the world. The other low-carbon energy sources have not had sufficient measurable research data from which it is possible to form a conclusion in terms of environmental impact.

Table 3.9 Other renewables—ocean, biomass, hydrogen and geothermal

Category	Environment and waste	Planning law	Finance	Safety
Is there a key issue?	Limited	No	Yes	?
Key issue	Impact on landscape and wildlife	Limited	Receive few financial incentives	It is debatable if there is has been sufficient research into safety issues to aid the formulation of legislation for these energy sources

Source Constructed by Author (2014)

All these energy sources do not produce CO_2 so are potential new forms of low-carbon energy. Currently, however, they receive little in subsidy support. These energy sources require further development of legislation, in particular to ensure safety legislation is adopted and practised.

3.3.6 Final Reflections

Understand and consider the following:

- **Compare and contrast different countries and their law and policy for low-carbon energy sources?**
- **Consider difference between the law for fossil fuel and low-carbon energy sources?**
- **Is law different for fossil fuel and low-carbon energy sources?**

3.4 Recommended Reading

1. Cook, H (2013) The law of nuclear energy. UK: Sweet & Maxwell
2. Gerrard, MB (ed) (2012) The law of clean energy: efficiency and re-newables. US: American Bar Association
3. Holwerda, M (2014) EU regulation of cross-border carbon capture and storage: legal issues under the directive on the geological storage of CO_2 in the light of primary EU law. Cambridge, United Kingdom: Intersentia
4. Lindøe, PH, Baram, M and Renn, O (eds) (2013) Risk governance of offshore oil and gas operations. New York, US: Cambridge University Press

5. Lyster, R and Bradbrook, A (2006) Energy law and the environment. Cambridge, UK: Cambridge University Press
6. Makuch, KE and Pereira, R (2012) Environmental and energy law. Oxford, UK: Wiley-Blackwell
7. McHarg, A, Barton, B, Bradbrook, A and Godden, L (2010) Property and the law in energy and natural resources. Oxford, United Kingdom: Oxford University Press
8. Taverne, BG (2008) Petroleum, industry, and governments: a study of the involvement of industry and governments in the production, and use of petroleum. London, UK: Wolters Kluwer
9. Wilde, M (2nd ed) (2013) Civil liability for environmental damage. A comparative analysis of law and policy in Europe and the US. London, UK: Wolters Kluwer
10. Zillman, DN, McHarg, A, Barrera-Hernandez, L and Bradbrook, A (eds) (2014) The law of energy underground: understanding new developments in subsurface production, transmission, and storage. Oxford, United Kingdom: Oxford University Press

References

Australian Government: Great Barrier Reef Marine Park Authority (2005) Measuring the economic and financial value of the Great Barrier Reef Marine Park. Access Economics Pty Limited, Queensland. http://www.gbrmpa.gov.au/__data/assets/pdf_file/0004/5584/gbrmpa_RP84_Measuring_The_Economic_And_Financial_Value_Of_The_GBRMP_2005.pdf. Accessed 18 Oct 2014
Brulle RJ (2014) Institutionalizing delay: foundation funding and the creation of US climate change counter-movement organizations. Clim Change 122:681–694
Burges Salmon (2013) Guaranteeing tax relief for decommissioning. Oil and gas connect. http://www.burgessalmon.com/Sectors/energy_and_utilities/Oil%20and%20Gas/Publications/Guaranteeing_tax_relief_for_decommissioning_what_will_it_mean.pdf. Accessed 18 Oct 2014
European Commission (2007) Commission communication of 10 January 2007: "renewable energy road map. Renewable energies in the 21st century: building a more sustainable future". Accessed 18 Oct 2014: [COM(2006) 848]
European Commission (2014) Connecting Europe facility. http://ec.europa.eu/energy/mff/facility/connecting_europe_en.htm. Accessed 18 Oct 2014
Global Subsidies Initiative (2010) Untold billions: fossil-fuel subsidies, their impacts and the path to reform. Available and last accessed 18 Oct 2014. www.iisd.org/gsi/sites/default/files/transparency_ffs.pdf. Accessed 30 Nov 2013
Heede R (2014) Tracing anthropogenic carbon dioxide and methane emissions to fossil fuel and cement producers 1854–2010. Clim Change 122:229–241
Heffron RJ (2012) A justification for redefining competition policy in the 21st century in the UK. Interdisc J Econ Bus Law 1(3):74–117
Heffron RJ (2013) Accommodating energy law within environmental law: an Irish exploration. Ir Plann Environ Law 20(2):56–64

Hertz N (2001) The silent takeover: global capitalism and the death of democracy. Arrow Books, London

IEA, OPEC, OECD, and World Bank Joint Report (2010) Analysis of the scope of energy subsidies and suggestions for the G-20 Initiative (June 2010). Available and last accessed 18 Oct 2014. www.iea.org/weo/docs/G20_Subsidy_Joint_Report.pdf. Accessed 12 Dec 2013

Ronne A (2013) The Danish transition from 100 % oil imports via 100 % indigenous production towards 100 % green energy. http://www.scottishconstitutionalfutures.org/Default.aspx?tabid=1712&articleType=ArticleView&articleId=268. Accessed 18 Oct 2014

Smith A (1776) An inquiry into the nature and cause of the wealth of nations, Book 1 (5th edn, annotated reprint, Methuen, London, 1904). http://www.econlib.org/library/Smith/smWN.html. Accessed 18 Oct 2014

The Guardian (Watts J) (2010) Three Gorges dam may force relocation of a further 300,000 people. http://www.theguardian.com/environment/2010/jan/22/wave-tidal-hydropower-water. Accessed 18 Oct 2014

Chapter 4
Energy Law Research and Conclusions

4.1 Conducting Comparative Energy Studies

4.1.1 Introduction to Comparative Energy Law Studies

Comparative energy studies are one of the main research methods in the study of energy law. Comparative legal analysis has a long tradition in legal studies going back to French legal thinkers in the sixteenth century. For a student to understand the approaches and different methods used, it is of value to read a text in the area such as *The Oxford Handbook of Comparative Law* edited by Reimann and Zimmermann (2006). In general, comparative legal analysis will be between countries and sector. In the rest of this sub-section, the energy law and policy of a number of countries will be briefly detailed and represents a starting point for further analysis by a student in energy law and policy.

4.1.2 Energy Law and the European Commission

The EU provides a very good setting for comparative energy law research. The EU began with the management of two energy sources—coal and nuclear energy. Comparative legal analysis can be completed on different energy sources and different EU countries. There are also the competing aims of the energy law and policy triangle for further comparative analysis between countries.

Energy law has gradually returned as a major legal area in the EU. Three successive reform packages, known as the First, Second and Third Energy Packages, have seen a process of development with initial opposition. A Fourth Energy Package expected.

Part of Sect. 4.3 is from an article entitled: Heffron (2013). Thanks are expressed to the publisher of this journal.

4.1.3 Energy Law and the US Federal Authority

The US is probably the country with longest history of energy law. Early legislation was in place for the coal sector in the 1800s. A problem in the US has always been the effectiveness of energy law. There is a complex federal legal system in place and this ensures, to some degree, slow change. However, in the energy sector it has been through the US Environmental Protection Agency (EPA) that the current President, Barack Obama, has had more success.

The Energy Policy Act of 2005 was the last major piece of energy legislation. This encourages the development of, specifically, nuclear power, with several forms of incentives introduced. These take the form of loan guarantees, carbon-free production tax credits, protection tax credits, and a new form of risk insurance for the first six reactors. The aim of the legislation is to move the US towards a national goal of energy independence with the aid of nuclear power. The 2005 Act also continued the Price-Anderson Act (as explained earlier in Table 2.4).

The Clean Air Act (1970) has had an impact on energy infrastructure development —owing in part to the 1990 Amendments and the finalised EPA 2011 Cross-State Air Pollution Rule (CSAPR). It has meant that many new coal plant applications have been withdrawn over the past decade. It was due to the inability at federal level to achieve legislative change that President Obama had to seek alternative methods of encouraging a low-carbon economy that will battle against the increase in CO_2 emissions. It is worth noting this was part of the election promise that Barack Obama made when seeking election. So through the EPA the Obama administration is finally achieving some of its policy aims on climate change.

4.1.4 Influence of EU and US on National Energy Law Across the World

The US and EU are two good cases to use in comparative energy legal analysis, for a number of reasons. First, they both have a Federal and Member State structure (note that the EU does use the term 'Federal' while the US does not use the term 'Member State').

Secondly, both the US and EU have very advanced and, in many cases through their States, quite innovative energy law. The energy law that emanates from the EU and US is followed and adopted to a certain level by many countries across the world. There are a number of prominent approaches in the EU. These generally are from the Nordic countries (Finland, Sweden, Denmark and Norway), Germany, France and the UK. In the US, there are also different approaches. These generally emanate from the East Coast through the PJM electricity market. PJM is a liberalised electricity market formed of 13 US states and the District of Columbia (PJM represents the first three member states: Pennsylvania, New Jersey, and Maryland). In addition, California, Georgia, Texas and occasionally some other southern states have different approaches to energy law.

Thirdly, both the EU and US are key promoters of new technology in the energy sector. Energy law is used to promote the growth of these new technologies and also to encourage the development of expertise on and manufacture of these new technologies. This technology is then exported, and hence also influences the development and similarity of energy law in other countries beyond the EU and US.

4.1.5 Divergence Between Federal and State Energy Law

There are several main differences between federal and state energy law in a federalist structured nation. As stated, this is most relevant in an EU and US context but it applies also to other countries. Australia, Canada, and Germany (to a certain level in terms of energy law) have federal/state type structures where there is a significant degree of autonomy in energy policy, although not to the same degree as in Member States of the EU and states in the US.

Federal authorities have a number of concerns that are of most importance. These include future policy aims, and the development of energy infrastructure—in particular for transmission and transport. In addition, the federal authority will aim to ensure there is a level playing field for each energy source subject to its future policy aims.

In contrast, the Member State has control over the operation of its own electricity market. It must decide on which energy sources to promote and which to incentivise so as to encourage future development of energy infrastructure and also innovation. The variation occurs because not all states have access to natural resources, to sufficient water supplies for hydropower and nuclear energy, to sufficient wind power, or to their own coastline in order to avail themselves of offshore energy infrastructure.

4.1.6 A Brief Analysis of Energy Law in Five Other Countries

Australia

This is now one of the more controversial countries as regards its energy law and policy, and it has always been reluctant to sign up to international treaties in the area. It is a country with major energy resources; however, these are mainly fossil fuel energy resources. It does have some uranium mines and it exports this uranium since it has no nuclear reactors itself. Its energy regulator was only fully established in 2010; prior to this it had existed in different forms. The state of New South Wales (NSW) provides a lead for other Australian states in terms of energy and environmental law development. Other Australian states continue to look to NSW for guidance on energy law and policy.

Australia introduced new energy law designed to reduce its CO_2 emissions; however it repealed this legislation in July 2014. Moreover, it has gone further to begin a new wave of fossil fuel extraction. It will export a significant amount of these fossil fuels to China and India.

The fossil fuel industry in Australia is heavily supported through direct legislation (and also through absence of legislation). In particular, this relates to the subsidies the industry receives through tax breaks. The subsidies that have been highlighted by a number of studies state that the fossil fuel industry receives the equivalent of $8.5 billion (Australian dollars) in subsidies annually through budgetary support and tax exemptions; in comparison, the low-carbon industry receives an estimated $200 million (OECD 2012).

Brazil

With an abundance of natural energy resources, Brazil, compared with other developing countries, is quite advanced in its energy policy. It has made significant progress in developing renewable energy, specifically in relation to ethanol and hydropower; the latter has a major role in its electricity mix (see Table 4.1).

Problems emerged when Brazil found significant reserves of oil (for example, the Lula oil field) in the early 2000s, having relied on imports previously. The sector remains in a development stage, and there are many problems in the management of the sector. The legislation introduced initially to manage the oil industry and ensure revenue from it has not been effective. For the Lula field it is worth noting that Bear Sterns stated that the revenue would be $25–60 billion depending on market prices (The Scotsman 2007); however, the costs could be as high as $50–100 billion (The USA Today 2007; Businessweek 2007).

Brazil's electricity mix is very oriented towards low-carbon, and this in terms of climate change mitigation is very positive. However, it needs to be placed in context with the overall level of energy consumption, where fossil fuels account for 60 % of consumption; see Table 4.2.

Table 4.1 Brazilian electricity generation Mix	Brazilian electricity generation mix (2013)
	Oil and other liquid fuels—2 %
	Natural gas—5 %
	Coal—1 %
	Hydroelectricity—82 %
	Nuclear—3 %
	Biomass—7 %

Source Author (2014) adapted from Brown (2014)

Table 4.2 Brazilian energy mix by consumption

Brazilian 2013 energy mix by consumption (fuel mix)
Oil and other liquid fuels—47 %
Natural gas—8 %
Coal—5 %
Hyrdoelectricity—35 %
Nuclear—1 %
Other renewables—4 %

Source Author (2014) adapted from US Energy Information Administration (2014a, b, c)

Canada

Quite advanced in its energy legislation, Canada is similar to the US and EU to some degree. It has one of the world's oldest energy regulators, the National Energy Regulator, which was established in 1959. Canada's electricity mix is shown in Table 4.3 and it is similar to Brazil in having a high level of hydroelectricity.

Canada was at one stage similar to Australia, in terms of quite progressively aiming to develop its low-carbon sector and reduce its carbon emissions. However, the election of a new government in 2006 has led to recent changes that have been more negative (see the earlier discussion in Chap. 3). Canada has returned to and promised more extraction of fossil fuels and there are also more plans to drill for and extract resources in the Arctic.

China

Energy law in China is a relatively new concern. Over the past decade pollution has affected a large part of the population who live in the cities. Due to growing public health concerns and the resulting costs to the public health system, China has begun to develop new energy law that is intended to encourage the growth of a low-carbon energy sector.

There is a large amount of new energy infrastructure planned and major investment in the national electricity grid. In terms of new energy infrastructure investment, there have been policies in place since 2012 aimed at seeing wind

Table 4.3 Canadian electricity mix 2012

Canada's electricity generation mix (2012)
Fossil fuels—23 %
Hydroelectricity—58 %
Nuclear—14 %
Wind—4 %
Other renewables—1 %

Source Author (2014) adapted from US Energy Information Administration (2014a, b, c)

power reach 100 GWe, solar power exceed 21 GWe and installed nuclear energy reach circa 40 GWe (see Chap. 2). China has also made major investments in energy resources and energy projects abroad. In the EU China has new plans to invest in Romania and the UK, both in the nuclear energy sector. Other investments worldwide are numerous and detailed in a comprehensive account by Dambisa Moyo (2012) in *Winner Take All: China's Race for Resources and What it Means For Us.*

India

India is in a similar situation to China in that it is planning to develop a significant amount of new energy infrastructure. However, unlike China, it is not as engaged in hedging its risk, and does not aim to develop its own energy expertise in all types of different energy infrastructure; nor does it actively pursue energy assets abroad or joint cooperation and ownership in energy projects abroad.

India does, however, have a surprisingly long history of energy law, which first emerged in the 1950s. However, its effectiveness is in question and particularly so over the past 20 years. The energy consumption mix and electricity mix are dominated by fossil fuels—see Table 4.4.

The electricity system in India is blighted by problems, with rolling blackouts sometimes lasting for several hours a day. Further, many fossil fuel plants are operating at only 70 % of their capacity. Overall, a major investment is needed in infrastructure in the electricity sector.

4.1.7 Final Reflections

Understand and consider the following:

- **Comparative energy law analysis involves identifying which approaches to energy law from which countries are:**
  - the most important (for the given research question)
  - most influential on the development of energy law
  - transferable in another jurisdiction.

- **It also involves identifying what the approach achieves (i.e. is the energy law successful in delivering its own aims?).**

Table 4.4 India's energy mix by consumption and electricity mix

Indian 2014 energy mix by consumption (fuel mix)	
Energy mix by consumption 2012	**Electricity mix (installed capacity) 2014**
Petroleum and other liquid—22 %	Coal 59 %
Natural gas—7 %	Natural gas 9 %
Coal—44 %	Diesel <1 %
Hydroelectricity 3 %	Hydroelectricity 16 %
Nuclear 1 %	Nuclear—2 %
Other renewables 1 %	Other renewables—13 %
Biomass and waste 22 %	

Source Author (2014) adapted from US Energy Information Administration (2014a, b, c)

4.2 Case Law in the Energy Sector

4.2.1 An Example of Case Law in the Energy Sector: The European Union

In general, case law in the energy sector in the EU has in the past focused on competition and more specifically Anti-Competitive Agreements (Art. 101 Treaty on the Functioning of the European Union—TFEU) and Abuse of Dominance (Art. 102 TFEU). For an explanation of these terms, see Table 4.5.

Table 4.5 EU competition definitions

I. Anti-competitive agreements (Art. 101 TFEU)
There are two forms of anti-competitive agreement:
1. Horizontal agreements—any arrangement between actual or potential competitors, operating at the same level of the production or distribution chain; and
2. Vertical agreements—any arrangement entered into between two or more firms, each of which operates at a different level of the production or distribution chain, and relating to the conditions under which said firms may purchase sell or resell certain goods or services
II. Abuse of dominance (Art. 102 TFEU)
This can be in the product market and/or the geographic market. There are two forms:
1. Exclusionary practices—imposing exclusive purchase commitments on customers; unfair or predatory pricing; refusal to supply; fidelity rebates and rebates with similar effects
2. Exploitative practices—unfair prices or trading condition (e.g. excessive pricing); discrimination/different sales conditions; and tying

The following are examples of some of the main cases decided upon by (or in agreement with) the European Commission (EC) related to the energy sector. These cases—Case Examples 1–5 in Table 4.6—demonstrate a range of scenarios and the possible solutions potentially available.

4.2.2 Examples of National Case Law

The EU energy sector has developed over the past two decades principally due to the First, Second and Third Energy Packages. A key development of these packages was to create a national energy regulator (NER). One of the functions that these NERs were responsible for was to enforce energy law at a national level. This remains the case.

Many NERs were created in the 1990s both before and after the first EU internal electricity market directive was approved. However, it was not until the second internal electricity and natural gas market directives (Directives 2003/54/EC and 2003/55/EC) that independent energy regulators became mandatory (Vasconcelos 2005). In contrast, independent regulators have been a feature in the US since the nineteenth century (in particular, in the railways sector) and in Canada, where the NER was established in 1959.

The second EU Energy Package (directives) facilitated more widespread cooperation between NERs and the European Commission. This has taken the form of unofficial cooperation and the establishment of the Council of European Energy Regulators (CEER) in 2000 and the European Regulators Group for Electricity and Gas (ERGEG) in 2003.

It was the third directive in the sector (the Third Energy Package) that was to resolve one of the main challenges remaining in the electricity sector. This was competition, and indeed Jorge Vasconcelos, the President of the Council of European Energy Regulators, believed that it was important to resolve market failures and that this could be achieved though cooperation between the Commission, National Competition Agencies (NCAs) and NERs:

> Therefore, co-operation between the European Commission, competition authorities and energy regulatory authorities (through ERGEG) is also very important as regards the definition of 'energy markets', the assessment of market power and effective competition and the definition of appropriate and anti-trust remedies (Vasconcelos 2005: 17).

The Third Energy Package has a number of specific aims at its core:

- it applies strict rules on unbundling of network operators;
- enforcement of intra-European co-operation; and
- the European Commission itself will make use of Art. 101 TFEU and Art. 102 TFEU (if the respective National Competition Agency has not acted).

Table 4.7 highlights a number of cases where recently NCAs have investigated certain firms, and applied action to correct the anti-competitive market behavior.

Table 4.6 EC competition cases in the energy sector

European commission: case example 1
Case name:
E.On/Gdf (Case COMP/39.401) commission decision of 8 July 2009 [2009] OJ C 248/5
Case background
In 1975, both companies had agreed to build the MEGAL pipeline together. They agreed to a market sharing agreement which they maintained despite the opening of the European gas markets to competition by Directive 98/30/EC
Outcome: financial penalty
The EC fined both companies €553 million in July 2009; however, this was later reduced to €320 million
European commission: case example 2
Case name:
Distrigaz, 2007—commission decision of COMP/B-1/37966—distrigaz, 11 October 2007
Case background
Market foreclosure concerns by the Commission were expressed due to the long-term gas supply contracts between Distrigaz, the Belgian incumbent national supplier, and its large gas contracts. The Commission stated that competing suppliers could be foreclosed because of:
• the duration of the contracts; and
• the volume of gas in control of Distrigaz which could impact upon other alternative suppliers building up a viable customer base
Outcome: restriction on trade
Commitment by distrigaz to:
• a minimum of 65 % (average 70 %) of gas supplied will return to the market (i.e. alternative suppliers can make competing offer);
• no new contracts can be longer than 5 years;
• no gas supply agreements with resellers longer than 2 years; and
• commitments have a duration of 4 years but will continue should Distrigaz have a market share of 40 % plus and 20 % more than its nearest competitor
European commission: case example 3
Case name:
GAS NATURAL/ENDESA—see commission press release IP/00/297

(continued)

Table 4.6 (continued)

European commission: case example 3

Case name:

GAS NATURAL/ENDESA—see commission press release IP/00/297

Case background

This was only a potential case for the European commission, and it was not pursued after the following actions listed below by the two parties. The relationship between GAS NATURAL (dominant company in the gas market) and ENDESA (dominant company in the electricity market) had raised the concerns of the Commission

Outcome: restriction on trade

Commitment by both companies to:

- reduce the gas volume covered by the contract so as to free part of ENDESA's purchasing capacity and force it to be a customer;

- a reduction of the duration of the supply contract by a third, hence, the contract will not exceed 12 years in normal delivery periods; and

- GAS NATURAL will not require ENDESA or any other electricity generator to use the gas for electricity generation purposes, hence ENDESA or other firms can resell the gas

European commission: case example 4

Case name:

EDF—see commission press release IP/10/290

Case background

Similar to the GAS NATURAL/ENDESA case, this was only a potential case for the European commission. It was not pursued after the following actions by EDF listed below

The commission had expressed concern in 2008 that EDF was abusing its dominant position in the French electricity market. Principally its supply contracts and restriction preventing customers reselling the electricity were identified as preventing new entrants to the market. For competition to develop, EDF's competitors needed access to the customers who were currently tied into long-term contracts

(continued)

Table 4.6 (continued)

European commission: case example 4
Case name:
EDF—see commission press release IP/10/290
Outcome: restriction on trade
Commitment by EDF to:
• average of 65 % of the electricity supplied to large customers will return to the market every year because the contract ends or customers can opt-out of contract for free (some flexibility given, but 60 % of EDF's total contracted electricity must return to the market);
• future new contracts can be no longer than 5 years, unless the customer can opt out for free after 5 years;
• EDF will offer customers non-exclusive contracts, so they can source part of their electricity need from other suppliers; and
• this commitment will have a duration of 10 years unless EDF's market share drops below 40 % for 2 years
European commission: case example 5
Case name:
CEZ, 2011—commission decision of COMP/39.727
Case background
The commission expressed concern that CEZ was preventing entry into the market for electricity generation and wholesale supply in the Czech electricity market. CEZ was apparently hoarding capacity in the transmission network, thereby disincentivising third parties from making new investments in new generation capacity
Outcome: divesting of an asset
Commitment by CEZ to:
• divest coal or lignite generation capacity (800–1,000 MW) which would immediately give a third party a significant presence (similar to 6 % of total generation capacity) on the Czech electricity market

Source Constructed by Author (2014)

Table 4.7 Examples of NCA cases: recent cases in the energy sector in the EU where national competition authorities intervened

NCAs continue to investigate the full range of competition issues in the energy sector, issuing financial penalties, making commitments by firms binding, and increasing their knowledge of certain sectors in sector inquiries

A. German supply contracts

The German NCA imposed remedies in the form of maximum durations on gas suppliers—maximum 2 years for purchasing obligations above 80 % of required volumes, and maximum 4 years for purchasing obligations of above 50–80 % of required volumes

See: Bundeskartellamt, B8—113/03–8—saar femgas AG, of 29 January 2007

B. Italian gas distribution

The Italian NCA fined two gas distributors nearly €5 million for an abuse of dominance. The NCA found that the two companies refused and then later delayed supplying information relating to the operation of the gas network so that municipalities awarding the next contract were delayed, and thus the two distributing companies where enabled to continue their contract with the said municipalities

December 2011 and January 2012—see www.agcm.it/en/newsroom/press-releases

In another case, the Italian NCA fined two gas distribution companies circa €1.3 million when they submitted joint offers for public tenders when both were capable of operating alone, and where they were the sole bidders for the contract. The NCA accused both companies of aiming to protect and continue their monopolies

2011—See www.agcm.it/en/newsroom/press-releases

C. Italian electricity balancing services

The Italian NCA fined three electricity producers for raising price levels in April–August 2010 through colluding on the offer of electricity balancing services to TERNA, the grid operator. These three companies were the only operators of power plants that could offer balancing services on weekends and public holidays in the Campania region. Significantly while there was no evidence of collusion or an actual agreement, it appeared that the three operators had agreed to manipulate their bids in a method that ensured they took turns in supplying electricity to the grid operator

2011—See www.agcm.it/en/newsroom/press-releases

D. Spanish electricity distribution

In 2012 Endesa in Spain was subject to a number of fining decisions by the Spanish NCA. One of these was because of a complex scenario where Endesa was accused of foreclosing the market on its competitors. Essentially it was using the information it acquired as an electricity distributor to inform itself as to the market for new electricity installations, and hence it knew where the new large customers would need a grid connection

European competition network Brief 2/2012; see http://ec.europa.eu/competition/ecn/

Source Author (2014) adapted from Reidlinger (2012)

It is evident from these cases that the NCAs are taking the lead role in the EU energy sector to enforce competition. NERs can continue to ensure the Third Energy Package is applied, with the NCA there to ensure that its legislative aims are being followed in terms of increasing competition and protecting the consumer. In this way, the activities of the NCAs and NERs can complement each other. This is particularly important in the EU where NERs are relatively new institutions and in a state of transition.

4.2.3 Final Reflections

Understand and consider the following:

- **Be able to give examples of case law for a number of countries**
- **What are the key themes or major issues from the case law in this section?**

4.3 Conclusion—Looking Forward

4.3.1 Progress Across the World

Energy law is not confined to the countries mentioned in this book but is being developed across the world. An examination of countries in the EU and a range of countries outside the EU demonstrates that the development of specific law in the energy sector has been, and is, a concern of many governments. The desire of many governments is to develop their energy sectors, to encourage investment in energy infrastructure and in many cases to take action against climate change. Indeed, this latter consideration is significant when one considers what some countries have shown can be achieved by having effective energy law, for example, the earlier mentioned case of Denmark.

As stated in a number of sub-sections above, it is important to remember the overlap between law and policy in considering energy issues. Energy policy is the driver of the legislation. In order to have effective energy policy, it is necessary to have the legislation to deliver it. This is particularly important to secure investment from the private sector in the various infrastructures and initiatives that a government may see as being instrumental in delivering the energy policy it has promoted. The delay of the path of the Energy Bill in the UK is an example where a government failed to clarify its exact energy policy and thus investors were unsure what commitment they could offer (Heffron 2013a).

Despite the lethargy that the UK Energy Bill (now the UK Energy Act 2013) experienced in the legislative process, it represents an important piece of legislation in an EU context. Already other Member States have expressed a desire to incorporate aspects of it into their legislation. The UK Energy Act 2013 is ambitious, and it has built upon 10 years of policy and legislative development (Heffron 2012). Under this Bill, the electricity system will be redesigned and the energy sector focused on developing low-carbon energy assets in the medium to long term. Of note is the long-term focus of the legislation and in general the eventual cross-party political support for the legislation. Further, in many respects the coalition government (Conservatives and Liberal Democrats) is building on the work of the previous Labour government.

4.3.2 The Power of Energy Law

In these difficult financial times, with many countries experiencing some of the deepest recessions in a century, the power of energy law should be recognised. In comparison to environmental law where EU Member States must follow the direction of the EU, a country has much more control in determining what energy law it can enact. An example of this is what Denmark has done, and what the UK plans to do. In both these cases, energy law favours particular energy sources, and encourages their development. Although this is perhaps contrary to EU competition principles, these countries do support other aims of the EU such as contributing towards energy security and the EU 2020 renewable energy policy targets.

Denmark is the leading example of the power of energy law in the EU. Its growth in domestic energy production was one phase, but the second phase has seen substantial subsidies given to the wind energy sector. The development of the wind energy sector, as highlighted in Table 4.8, clearly demonstrates that with effective energy legislation, energy law can make a number of major contributions to a nation economically and environmentally. It also shows the period needed to develop an effective and sustainable energy value chain—i.e. the 35–40 years before Denmark witnessed the fruition of its wind energy industry.

What is clear from the Denmark case is the importance of policy formulation: all politicians, independent of their party, meet in a forum where energy policy for the

Table 4.8 The growth of the wind energy sector in Denmark	Key facts on the wind energy industry in Denmark
	• Installed capacity = 3,124 MW (2007)—423 MW is offshore
	• Wind power generates 20 % of electricity production (2007)
	• The Danish wind turbine industry employs 28,000 persons and sells turbines for €7 billion (2008)
	• Most of the turbines are exported and the Danish wind turbine industry serves 30 % of the world market (2007)
	Source Author (2014) adapted from Ronne (2013)

nation is agreed upon for the medium to long term. This has a number of benefits, with the most significant being to ensure private sector investment, with legal certainty providing stability for private investment. Uniquely, however, Denmark's energy policy also incorporates clear incentives for the public and encourages to a degree the need for the public to be involved in the decision-making and the potential for shared public–private ownership of energy assets. The net result thereof is that energy prices are lower for consumers.

4.3.3 Targeted Energy Legislation

A further demonstration of the autonomy and resulting power of energy law is the positive effect from *targeted legislation*. This book advances a theory of targeted legislation in energy law. Targeted legislation in the energy sector can have a significant effect in that it can be the deciding factor in whether or not energy infrastructure is developed. As a result, targeted legislation represents one way of directly contributing to climate change mitigation and reducing CO_2 emissions. Consequently it represents more of a hope in the battle against climate change than many environmental legislative initiatives (Heffron 2013b).

For example, in the US, the introduction of the Georgia Nuclear Energy Financing Act in 2009 was a key reason why the two-reactor nuclear energy project progressed (Heffron 2013c, d). This $16 billion nuclear energy project means a significant amount to the state of Georgia (population 9.9 million) (US Census Data 2013) in terms of job creation and resulting economic benefits. Further, the same is the case in the neighbouring state of South Carolina which has a similar project (V. C. Summer) underway after the introduction of similar legislation. Despite the economic crisis, these states have found a way to initiate these two low-carbon energy projects.

Other examples of targeted legislation have seen major developments that can directly contribute to reducing the effects of climate change. A further example in the US is where the EPA, given significant power to set air quality standards, has been responsible for a dramatic decrease in the number of coal-fired plant applications over the past 15-year period—from around 300 to just a few (Cleveland 2013). And through this legislation the EPA has closed down many coal-fired plants with more closures to follow. In the UK, a new development has seen the creation through legislation of new public administration units to directly oversee the development of new energy infrastructure—the Office for Nuclear Development and the Office for Unconventional Oil and Gas. These two units will oversee the delivery of new infrastructure in the nuclear and unconventional oil and gas sectors and will in essence create the legislation needed to do so. The targeted legislation that saw the development of and responsibilities given to these agencies will result in major transformation of these industrial sectors.

4.3.4 Conclusion

Energy law is back on the agenda across the world, and in particular in Europe, after previously having played a founding role in the creation of the European Community after the Second World War. In legal practice and in academia energy law has returned as a subject in its own right. This is in part due to the numerous reasons outlined earlier in this text but a key aspect is the realisation of the value of the energy sector to the economy during this time of deep and continuing economic crisis.

Energy law can be a powerful source of remodelling for the energy sector and for ensuring that there is continued investment in new energy infrastructure and in research and development. These two areas can directly contribute to reducing the effects of climate change by promoting and realising investment and construction in new low-carbon energy assets. In this way, energy law can complement the aims of environmental law. Further, in contrast to environmental law, energy law can, in the form of targeted legislation, directly support and encourage specific new low-carbon infrastructure initiatives.

The EU is fast becoming the global leader in the development of energy law; this is in part driven by the European Commission and in part by the autonomy of EU Member States to develop their own energy law. Over the last decade, the European Commission has driven reform in the area. Its focus has been on increasing transparency and competition into the energy sector. New regulations are in place for enabling EU national energy regulators to enforce these two latter aims. There are also policy issues such as those for climate change and energy security which EU Member State governments are required to adhere to. In addition to reformed energy regulators, new public institutions that act as project managers in terms of delivering policy can assist in the creation of a low-carbon economy. These new initiatives by the European Commission and the associated energy law developed by EU Member States highlight the possibilities for achievement that countries can aspire to.

It is possible to enact energy law that embraces vision, ambition and imagination in delivering a long-term energy policy. More action is needed by individual countries to achieve cross-institutional and political involvement and cooperation in ensuring a deliverable energy policy. In this context, planning legislation for new energy infrastructure projects needs to begin well in advance, while incentives for the development of low-carbon energy infrastructure need to be legislated for quickly so as to encourage investment by the private sector.

4.3.5 Final Reflections

Understand and consider the following:

- **How is energy law effective?**
- **What might be the future direction of energy law internationally and at a national level giving examples from several countries?**

4.4 Recommended Readings

1. Bjørnebye, H (2010) Investing in EU energy security: exploring the regulatory approach to tomorrow's electricity production. London, UK: Wolters Kluwer
2. Dreger, J (2014) The European Commission's energy and climate policy: a climate for expertise? Basingstoke: Palgrave Macmillan
3. Freeman, J and Gerrard, MB (2nd ed) (2014) Global climate change and US law. US: American Bar Association
4. Glachant, M Finon, D and De Hautecloque, A (eds) 2011 Competition, contracts and electricity markets: a new perspective. Cheltenham, UK: Edward Elgar
5. Glachant, M, Hallack, M and Vazquez (2013) Building competitive gas markets in the EU: regulation, supply and demand. Cheltenham, UK: Edward Elgar
6. Kramer, AS and Fusaro, PC (eds) (2010) Energy and environmental project finance law and taxation: new investment techniques. New York, US: Oxford University Press
7. Metcalf, GE (ed) (2014) US energy tax policy. New York, US: Cambridge University Press
8. Roe, T and Happold, H (Dingemans, J—consultant editor) (2011) Settlement of investment disputes under the Energy Charter Treaty. Cambridge-New York: Cambridge University Press
9. Roggenkamp, MM., Barrera-Hernandez, L, Zillman, DN and Del Gyayo, I (eds) (2012) Energy networks and the law: innovative solutions in changing Markets. Oxford, United Kingdom: Oxford University Press
10. Zillman, DN, Redgwell, C and Barrera-Hernandez, L (2008) Beyond the carbon economy: energy law in transition. Oxford, United Kingdom: Oxford University Press

References

Brown A (2014) Evolution of Brazilian electricity market. World Bank/ NEW Seminar 17 January 2014, Beijing, China. http://www.hks.harvard.edu/hepg/Papers/2014/World%20Bank% 20China%20Jan%2017%202014.pdf. Accessed 18 Oct 2014

Businessweek (2007) Offshore oil discovery could make Brazil major energy exporter. 11 Sept 2007. http://www.businessweek.com/stories/2007-11-19/brazil-the-new-oil-superpowerbusinessweek-business-news-stock-market-and-financial-advice. Accessed 18 Oct 2014

Cleveland S (2013) Getting gas right: navigating the shale boom to reap the most benefits for the climate. In: International Conference on "policy delivery on low carbon energy generation infrastructure in the UK", University of Stirling, Scotland, UK, 5 April 2013. http://www.stir.ac.uk/cehp/newsandevents/policy-delivery/. Accessed 18 Oct 2014

Heffron RJ (2012) Lessons from the United States: for legal change and delay in energy law in the United Kingdom. Int Energy Law Rev 31(2):71–77 (Discusses the path to the development of the UK Energy Bill 2013)

Heffron RJ (2013) Accommodating energy law within environmental law: an Irish exploration. Ir Planning Environ Law 20(2):56–64

Heffron RJ (2013a) The application of contrast explanation to energy policy research: UK nuclear energy policy 2002–2012. Energy Policy 55:602–616 (Discusses the path to the development of the UK Energy Bill 2013)

Heffron RJ (2013b) Targeted legislation: the saviour of climate change mitigation. Chevening Global Environmental Event, Edinburgh School of Law, University of Edinburgh, Scotland

Heffron RJ (2013c) Lessons for nuclear new build in the USA 1990–2010: a three state analysis. Technol Forecast Soc Change 80(5):876–892

Heffron RJ (2013d) Nuclear energy policy in the United States 1990–2010: a federal or state responsibility. Electricity Policy Research Working Paper Series, EPRG WP 1301. University of Cambridge, Cambridge

Moyo D (2012) Winner take all: China's race for resources and what it means for us. Penguin Books, London

OECD (2012) Inventory of estimated budgetary support and tax expenditures for fossil fuels 2013. OECD, Paris

Reidlinger A (2012) Competition law enforcement in the energy sectors by the European Commission. In: Conference on 'Energy community seminar on competition law enforcement'. Austria, Vienna

Reimann M and Zimmermann R (Eds) (2006) The oxford handbook of comparative law. Oxford University Press, Oxford

Ronne A (2013) The Danish transition from 100 % oil imports via 100 % indigenous production towards 100 % green energy. http://www.scottishconstitutionalfutures.org/Default.aspx?tabid= 1712&articleType=ArticleView&articleId=268. Accessed 18 Oct 2014

The Scotsman (2007) Over a barrel. 10 Nov 2007. http://www.scotsman.com/business/energy/over-a-barrel-1-1427299. Accessed 18 Oct 2014

The USA Today (2007) Brazil, the new oil superpower. http://usatoday30.usatoday.com/money/industries/energy/2007-11-09-brazil-oil_N.htm. Accessed 18 Oct 2014

US Census Bureau (2013) United States Census Bureau People QuickFacts. http://quickfacts.census.gov/qfd/states/13000.html. Accessed 18 Oct 2014

US Energy Information Administration (2014) Brazil. http://www.eia.gov/countries/cab.cfm?fips= br. Accessed 18 Oct 2014

US Energy Information Administration (2014) Canada. http://www.eia.gov/countries/country-data.cfm?fips=CA&trk=m. Accessed 18 Oct 2014

US Energy Information Administration (2014) India. http://www.eia.gov/countries/cab.cfm?fips= in. Accessed 18 Oct 2014

Vasconcelos J (2005) Towards the internal energy market: how to bridge a regulatory gap and build a regulatory framework. Eur Rev Energ Markets 1(1):1–17